Story of Down Under

History of Australia in Cartoons: A Laugh-Out-Loud Trip Through Time

Written by Lachlan Lancelot & Illustrated by Longge Li

Copyright © 2025 by Lachlan Lancelot.

All rights reserved.

No portion of this book may be reproduced in any form without written permission from the publisher or author except as permitted by copyright law.

Cover by Longge Li.

Illustrations by Longge Li.

Special thanks to Mr JMD

Table of contents

Introduction...6

Chapter1: Aboriginal People..9

Chapter2: Life in Australia... 25

Chapter3: Cook and Banks... 56

Chapter4: The First Fleet... 114

Chapter5: Tough Times in NSW......................................136

Chapter6: Hunter VS Macarthur.....................................158

Chapter7: King VS Macarthur.. 176

Chapter8: Legendary Bligh..194

Chapter9: The Father of Australia................................. 210

Thank you !... 224

Introduction

I wanted to impress people.

You know, drop some fancy historical facts at a party, maybe sound deep, mysterious, even a little cultured.

So, I thought, 'Hey, why not study history?'

Big mistake.

Turns out, history books are dry — like, Sahara Desert dry. Reading them felt like chewing on sandpaper while someone whispered dates at me.

I thought, enough of this. I will make history fun and easy to read.

I designed this book to be your new go-to. Instead of mindlessly swiping your phone, it's perfect for killing time while you're waiting for public transport or… taking care of the *morning duty*.

Waiting for public transport.   Taking care of the morning duty.

This book is your secret weapon for casually dropping, 'Oh, by the way, did you know…' at just the right moment — whether you're strolling through a museum, stuck on a school trip, or watching a film with friends. You'll be ready to impress your crush, your mates, or even your mate's girlfriend…

I'll take you through major moments in Australian history — from the ancient Aboriginal times to British colonisation.

But hang on — this isn't your secondary school history class. If you're after deep academic essays and footnotes, you might want to look elsewhere. This ride's a bit more fun (and a lot less formal).

This is a cartooned, cheeky, no-snore-zone guide to Australia's past. With jokes and personality, like a stand-up comedy show.

Written by a regular guy who just loves a good laugh while learning something worth knowing.

Meet the creators of this book

Lachlan Lancelot.

*A very average Aussie bloke with a dad bod and a white belt in Brazilian Jiu-Jitsu.
He's got heart and zero winning record.*

Longge Li.

*A tiny Asian man, armed with a purple belt in Brazilian Jiu-Jitsu.
He draws.
He chokes.
He brings the funny.*

Together, we're here to serve up facts with a side of chuckles.

So, buckle up, flip the page, and let's make history something worth bragging about.

CHAPTER 1
Aboriginal People

Around 60,000 to 70,000 years ago (historians still debate the exact timeline — but honestly who cares) people came from Asia and arrived at the Australian continent.

Back then, the world looked pretty different. Sea levels were about 120 metres lower, so a lot of what's now ocean was dry land. Instead of massive ocean crossings, they could island-hop their way to Australia.

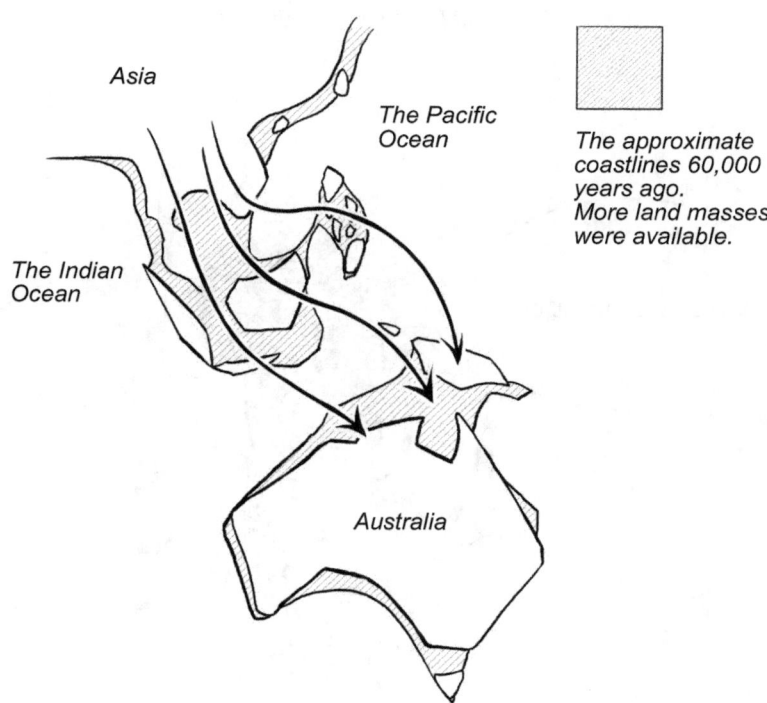

These early explorers used simple materials like bamboo rafts — or really, anything that floated — to make their way across the waters.

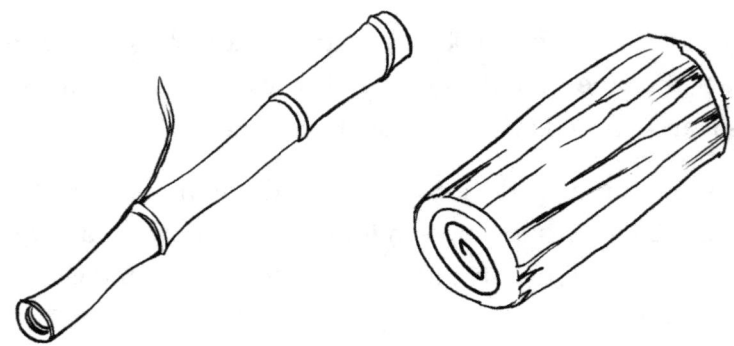

Any floating material they can find.

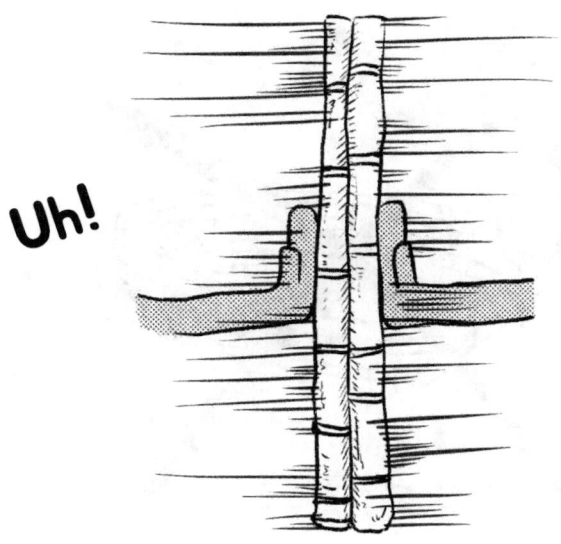

A bamboo raft!

Woops not like this.

Something more like this!

Why did they leave Asia and take such a big risk to travel?

Well, some historians think they might have been the losers of tribal battles. They got kicked out and had to go find a new home across the sea.

Two tribes fought.

And one tribe lost.

The winner takes all.

So, they had no choice but to take the risk — paddling across the ocean in search of land, food, and a fresh start.

Eventually, they made it to the Australian continent.

Back then, Australia was crawling with massive animals.

What did they find?

Wombats the size of a car.

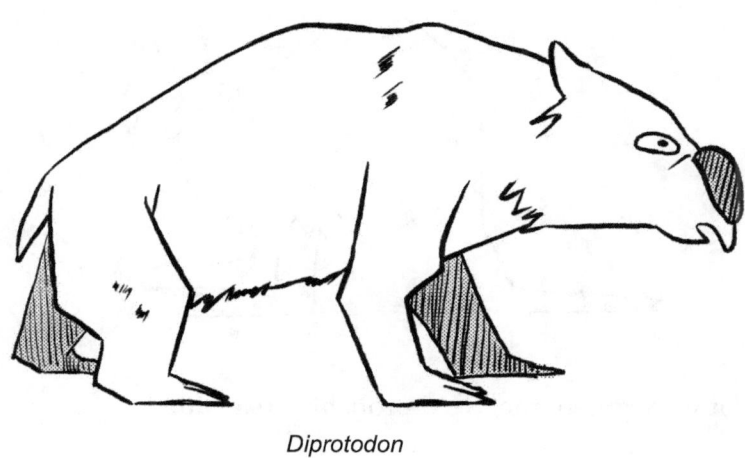

Diprotodon

Lizards longer than your dining table.

Giant kangaroos that could dunk on an NBA player.

If it were you or me, we'd probably be terrified.

But for them?

The big animals were perfect for their empty stomachs.

Unfortunately for the animals, people were *really* hungry.

Historians believe, this is the main reason those giant creatures went extinct — they were hunted into oblivion.

CHAPTER 2
Life in Australia

Property

The Aboriginal people didn't have the concept of ownership like we do today.

They were nomadic — constantly moving with the seasons and food supply.

Instead of carrying their stuff around with them, they just left tools behind.

Knowing that when they returned, they could just pick them up again.

It was like prehistoric Airbnb, but for tools.

Battles

Battles between tribes were a part of life.

Sometimes they fought over territory, food, or someone's belief. (Hmm, sounds a bit like modern-day politics.)

When a fight broke out, it didn't just end there, revenge would follow. A strong 'eye for an eye' mentality kept the cycle going, with each side seeking to get even.

Marriage and family

Often, a man could have multiple wives.

Why? Because survival was hard.

If a man died in a hunt or fight (and many did), another man would take care of his wives and kids.

It was about protection and survival — not romance.

Hunting for meat

Death from hunting

Fighting another man

Death from fighting

A 'good' man wasn't just someone with strength or charm — he needed to have hunting and fighting skills.

He had to be able to offer a reliable food source and protection.

For women, the expectations were different but just as essential. A desirable woman was someone who is able to give birth and raise children.

And the ability to gather food — like nuts, fruits, roots, and other edible plants — was essential for survival, especially when Daddy went out hunting and ended up as dinner for the animal he was after.

What's really interesting is that women were the main food providers, since hunting wasn't exactly a guaranteed success — boomerangs don't always come back with dinner, and neither did the men! Women would gather nuts, fruits and other vegetables for the family.

It's estimated that 70–80% of the family food came from what the women collected.

In the Aboriginal community, everyone had a role to play.

Husbands hunted, wives gathered — and if you messed with the missus, you didn't just miss dinner. You risked the whole family going on a surprise fasting season.

Diet

Aboriginal people had a pretty epic menu.

They feasted on kangaroos, emus, fish, shellfish, bush fruits, wattle seed, native herbs, and even reptiles.

The *Witchetty grub* is one of the most well-known and important bush foods in Aboriginal culture. Highly nutritious and rich in protein, fats, and carbohydrates, it was a vital food source — especially in tough conditions.

These grubs were often eaten raw, but could also be cooked for a softer, creamier texture.

In some regions Aboriginals also used to eat a big moth called the *Bogong Moth*, about the size of your hand.

These moths would migrate in huge numbers, making them an easy and reliable food source.

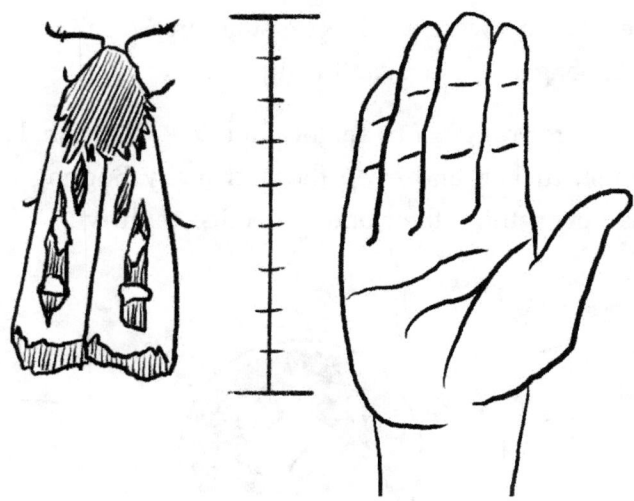

Apparently, when baked, they smelled like nuts — nature's original energy bars. 100% organic, straight from the source.

The Aboriginal diet was packed with nutrition, and historians say people at the time were eating far better than the Europeans, who were stuck with stale bread, salted meat, and boiled cabbage. You just can't compare.

With a diverse range of fresh, local foods — like fish, kangaroo, nuts, bush tucker, and even those crunchy Bogong moths — they had everything their bodies needed to thrive.

Dingo

Dingos came to Australia and quickly became man's best friend.

So, what's a dingo? In short, they're a unique type of dog with wolf-like traits.

They hunt in packs, don't bark like regular dogs, but they make a high-pitched, eerie howl, like that of a wolf.

Oh, and they've got incredibly nimble joints, making them great hunters.

Although dingoes are considered an iconic Australian native animal, they didn't originate here. Dingoes aren't native to the Australian continent in the same way kangaroos or emus are.

Just like the First Australians, dingoes came from another continent — yep, you guessed it: Asia! They were brought over around 4,000 years ago, making them about as old as Chinese history.

The relationship between people and dingoes was like the classic Japanese anime *Pokémon*.

People would catch wild dingoes — often by stealing pups straight from the pack — and then raise and train them to live alongside humans. (No *Poké Balls* involved, though.)

And just like in the anime, they hunted together.

They ate together, slept together and survived together.

It was a bond built on survival, trust, and teamwork.

But unlike the anime, if they didn't catch food then…

The dingo *became* food.

Yes, dingos were also people's emergency food.

The bond between humans and dingoes wasn't just about companionship — it was also about keeping each other alive (well, it was mostly to keep the humans alive).

Leisure activities and inventions

When the whole food problem is taken care of, people could focus on other things. Like painting.

The aboriginal people used to paint *a lot*.

They painted on cave walls…

Rocks, pebbles…

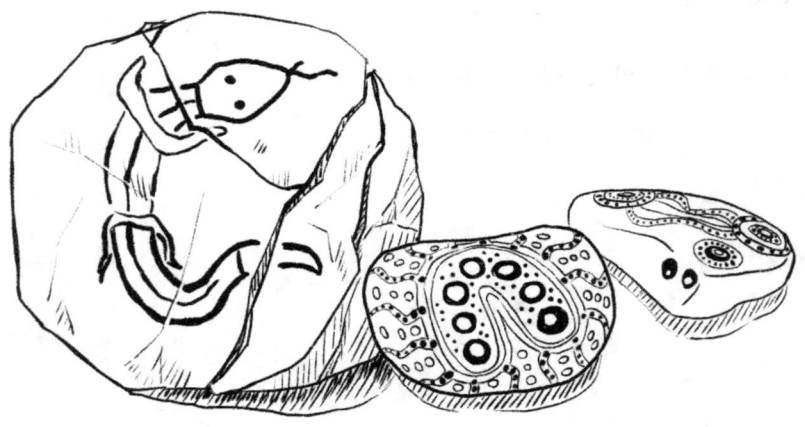

And on each other!

And even on their weapons too!

When it comes to inventions, the *boomerang* stands out the most, and it turns out, there's more than one kind.

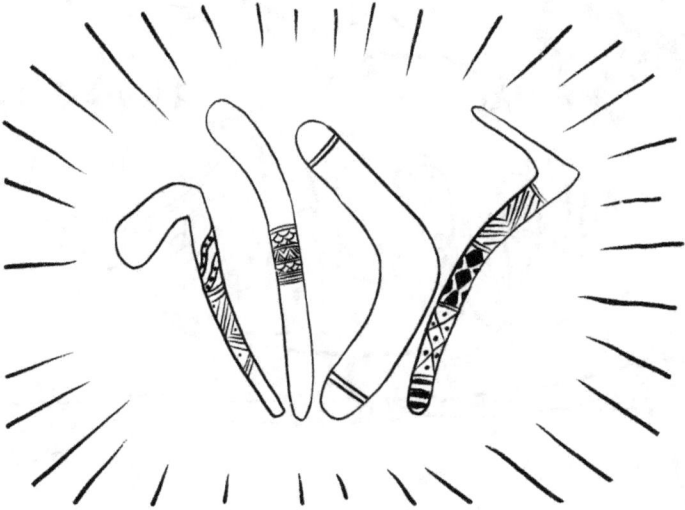

Boomerangs were used to catch birds…

And for clubbing people... enemies... or maybe an annoying neighbour. Just give it a whack!

Trade

The Aboriginals traded with the Makassar who were people from Indonesia, who were *crazy* about sea cucumbers — also known as *Trepang* — found along Australia's coasts.

The Aboriginal people traded sea cucumbers, and in return they got things like fabric, tobacco, smoking pipes, and shiny metal tools — like axes and knives.

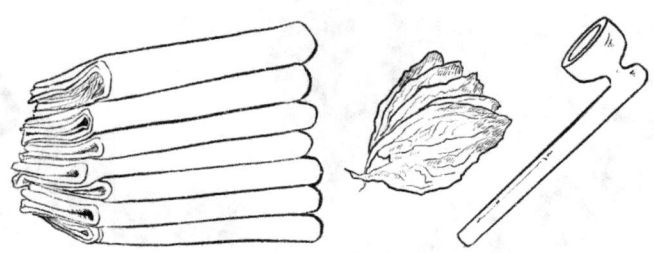

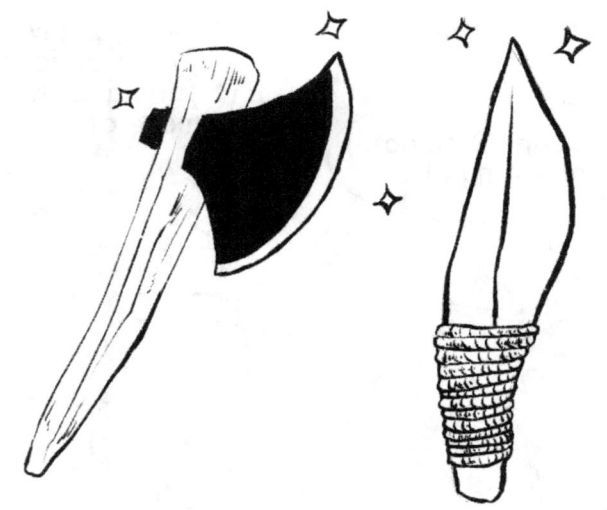

Axe — easy to chop wood *Knife — easy to stab people*

They even introduced the Van Dyke beard style.

Aboriginal people in some regions may have looked like this.

The Aboriginals also traded among themselves across different tribes. For example, some swapped pretty shells for possum skins.

Religion

The *Dreamtime* is the myth and religion that Aboriginal people believed in and different regions had their own rituals and legends. In simple terms, it goes like this:

The world began in total darkness.

Then, as the land started to form, *spiritual beings* emerged — taking the form of humans, animals, or supernatural creatures.

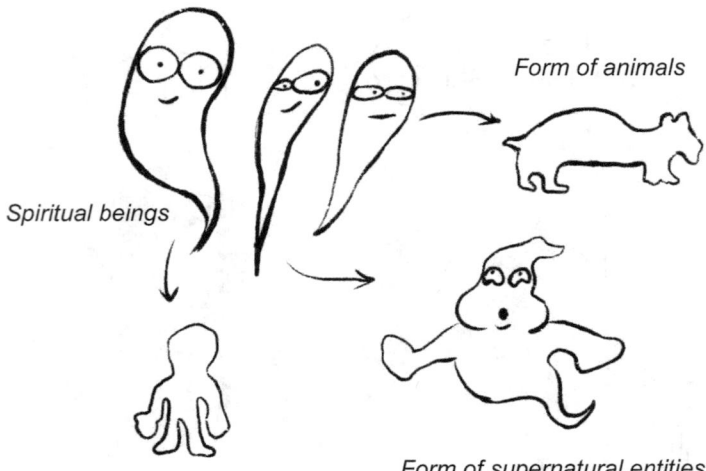

Spiritual beings

Form of animals

Form of humans

Form of supernatural entities

These beings travelled across the land, creating mountains, rivers, animals, people, and sacred places along the way. The paths they took were called *Songlines*.

Songlines

Songlines are like spiritual maps of the land. They're not just physical routes — but stories that connect Aboriginal people to their ancestors, their land, and each other.

Since Aboriginal people didn't have a written language, they passed these stories down through songs, dances, ceremonies, and oral storytelling.

One of the most famous Dreamtime stories is the tale of the *Rainbow Serpent*. This huge, colourful spirit-being is said to have slithered across the land in ancient times.

The Rainbow Serpent is said to have emerged from the earth during the Dreamtime.

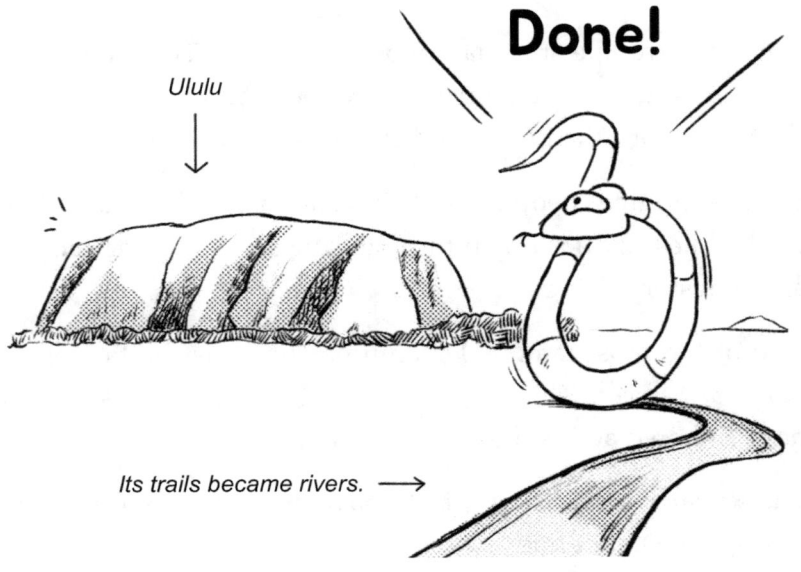

As it moved, it shaped the landscape creating rivers, valleys, and even *Uluru*. (A single, giant rock — not a mountain, a rock).

In some versions, the Rainbow Serpent brings life and fertility. In others, it punishes those who break sacred laws. So yeah — the Rainbow Serpent is almighty.

The Dreamtime isn't just a religion. It's a way of life. It tells people who they are, where they come from, and how they should care for the land around them.

For over 60,000 years, Aboriginal people lived by these stories — peaceful, steady, and thriving.

Then — *boom!* — out of nowhere, their worst enemy appeared: white people.

From the next chapter, it's our story!

CHAPTER 3
Cook and Banks

In the 18th century, James Cook was born into a poor farming family; his early life rooted in the simplicity of rural England.

He was one of the lucky ones who got a chance to attend school. Although he didn't stay long, he had a passion for math and mapping.

Then at 18, he joined a merchant shipping company, where he learned navigation and seamanship.

Later, he joined the Royal Navy just as the *Seven Years' War* broke out in Europe.

That war gave him a chance to show off his true skill: drawing super-accurate maps. Eventually he began to attract attention.

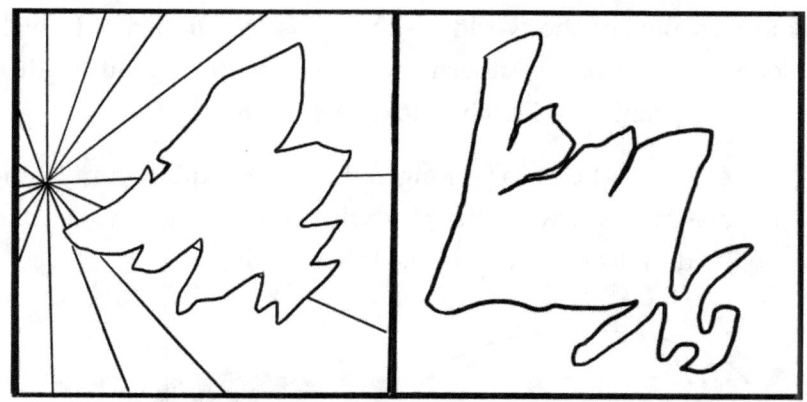

This is the same map of Newfoundland charted by James Cook, and it looks almost identical to Google Maps.

This is the map of Newfoundland charted by Nicolas Bellin in 1744.

After the Seven Years' War, Britain came out on top — it had beaten France, grabbed more territory, and felt like a global boss.

And with great victory... comes an inflated ego. Britain got itchy to conquer more stuff.

Britain wanted more trade routes and resources, spices, gold, fertile land, exotic goods... anything they could ship home and sell.

But Spain already had most of South America. The Dutch controlled Indonesia and parts of the Indian Ocean, and France was lurking in the Pacific too.

So, Britain became eager to find new, undiscovered territory where they could plant their flag and set up exclusive trade routes.

They were convinced there was an unknown continent in the southern part of the world — *Terra Australis Incognita* (which means 'mysterious southern land') — and they really didn't want the Spanish or Dutch to take over there first.

Now, if I were the boss picking someone to explore a mysterious new land, I'd want the guy who could draw an accurate map. And that's why they chose James Cook.

But here's the twist — the real mission was top secret.

The British government didn't tell anyone. James Cook included!

Officially he was told, 'Sail to Tahiti and observe the Transit of Venus.'

The Transit of Venus is when the planet Venus passes directly between the Earth and the Sun, super rare and a big deal for astronomers trying to measure the distance between Earth and the Sun.

Tahiti is a small island in the middle of the Pacific, and it was the perfect spot to watch the Transit of Venus.

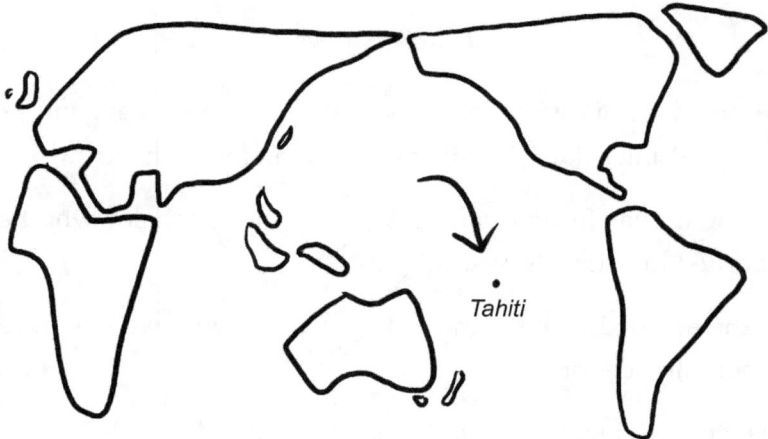

James Cook was promoted to lieutenant and made captain of HMS *Endeavour* — short for 'His' or 'Her' Majesty's Ship, depending on whether the ruler was a king or queen.

HMS Endeavour

He prepared his stuff – and his staff – for the voyage, and just before setting sail for Tahiti, a young man joined his crew.

That man was Joseph Banks. A young, rich bachelor who had inherited his father's wealth.

By the age of 25, he had already achieved what we like to call 'economic freedom'.

His annual income back then was around £10,000, which would be about £2–3 million today.

Banks was completely obsessed with plants and animals. He was the guy at the party who couldn't stop talking about his garden.

Somehow, he heard about Cook's mission to Tahiti and immediately wanted in — probably hoping to discover exotic species and bring back a few trophies for his garden.

Being rich, he could afford to indulge his hobby, so he went and knocked on Cook's door.

The *Endeavour* was already crammed with 80 to 90 people — naval officers, sailors, marines, and a handful of specialists like a surgeon, a cook (not James Cook, just the guy who made dinner), and a carpenter.

It wasn't a big ship, so James Cook was hesitant about taking on anyone else.

But Joseph Banks wasn't just anyone.

He used his social status to pull strings and pretty much forced Cook to accept him on board.

Joseph Banks, being a rich guy wouldn't just get on board a ship without his entourage.

He significantly expanded the number of crew by bringing his own team, which included Daniel Solander (a Swedish naturalist and Banks's close buddy), artists, assistants and servants.

The whole team squeezed into the already cramped *Endeavour*.

Altogether, Banks's party added about a dozen or more people to the crew, pushing the total number aboard the *Endeavour* to around 94 to 100 when they departed in August 1768.

Sailors' Utopia

They arrived in Tahiti, and Tahiti was fun!

Ah, Tahiti! A paradise brimming with tropical fruits and stunningly built people.

The crew of the *Endeavour* didn't just enjoy the food; they also took a keen interest in the company of the island's women.

The Polynesians, as we call them, were open-minded, and the island, lacking metal, was fascinated by anything shiny, especially nails.

Naturally, the sailors saw an opportunity.

They went wild, stealing nails from their own ship to trade for a night of... well, let's just say 'hospitality.'

Turns out, the island's men were just as eager for the shiny metal. So, it wasn't just the women getting traded for nails, everyone was getting in on the action!

It got so out of hand; they eventually stole everything — until there wasn't a single nail left on the ship. This became a serious problem since nails were crucial for the ship's maintenance. No nails = no safe voyage.

To make matters worse, the locals had a habit of stealing too. Many personal belongings were taken from the ship, and Cook began to worry that the gear needed to observe the Venus Transit might vanish next.

So, to keep things under control, he had to get tough, imposing flogging on both his own men (who couldn't resist stealing nails), and on Tahitians caught sneaking off with items from the ship.

Fortunately, the Transit of Venus was successfully recorded. It was supposed to be a major milestone in human history…

But for the sake of this book, I'll spare you the details. (Google it if you're really curious!)

Meanwhile Banks and his crew were also enjoying the intimate company of the local people.

Banks and Dr. Solander also busied themselves collecting all sorts of new species and samples.

Joseph Banks somehow convinced two Tahitian men, Tupaia and his servant Taiata, to join the *Endeavour*.

He wasn't just keen to show them the world, he also wanted to show the world them.

Tupaia was a superstar priest and navigator, kind of a big deal in the Pacific. But after some political drama and falling out with local chiefs in Tahiti, he figured, 'Why not hop on a ship and see the world?'.

Staying put wasn't exactly safe, so joining the voyage was part escape plan, part adventure.

Afterward, Cook thought his mission was done and began preparing to sail home.

Little did he know… the real adventure was just beginning.

The Secret Mission

As Cook was about to head back to his wife Elizabeth (and whether he stayed faithful to her in Tahiti is anyone's guess. What do you think?), he suddenly remembered something important.

He had been given a letter from his boss, with strict instructions to open it only after the Transit of Venus was observed.

In the letter, Cook discovered the truth! His real mission was to head south and search for the fabled land of *Terra Australis Incognita*. At the time was known as *New Holland* (The Dutch were big fans of slapping 'New' on places they found, like New Zealand and New Amsterdam).

So off Cook and the Endeavour went, heading into the unknown.

A whole new world

The Endeavour sailed south for two long months, and finally, they arrived at... New Zealand! Yep, not Australia.

They accidentally landed in New Zealand, which had been first discovered in 1642 by a Dutchman (who named it New Zealand), but most of it was still uncharted and unexplored.

As the *Endeavour* approached the bay, massive Māori canoes came toward the ship.

Cook was impressed! The canoes were massive, each holding around 30 men, and the Māori warriors were absolutely shredded.

Cook wondered what would happen.

He sent two small boats to shore, hoping for a peaceful chat. But things went downhill fast.

One boat got intercepted by a Māori canoe.

The British sailors freaked out, thinking they were under attack.

The second boat rushed in, and before anyone could say, *'Let's talk this out'* (and even if someone did, no one would've understood them anyway), chaos exploded.

In their panic, the British opened fire, and tragically, one Māori man was shot and killed.

Spears flew back in retaliation, but they didn't reach the boats.

Both sides retreated, tense and unsure of what just happened.

The next day, Cook tried again, but this time, he brought in his secret weapon, Tupaia.

Tupaia stepped onto shore with a group of marines, and *surprise!* He could actually talk to the Māori.

Their languages were surprisingly similar, and they even shared tattoo traditions.

This moment sparked a major theory. That perhaps the Māori had migrated from the Polynesian Islands, just like Tupaia. It was the first real clue that the Pacific was far more connected than the Europeans had ever imagined.

Even though they could communicate, it didn't exactly mean peace was on the horizon.

A few misunderstandings later, and both sides were back at it. Cook's men opened fire again, and several Māori were killed that day.

Definitely not the friendly welcome Cook was hoping for!

Cook and Banks eventually made it back to the ship, both feeling disappointed — maybe even a little guilty — about how things had gone.

To mark the less-than-warm reception, Cook named the spot: Poverty Bay.

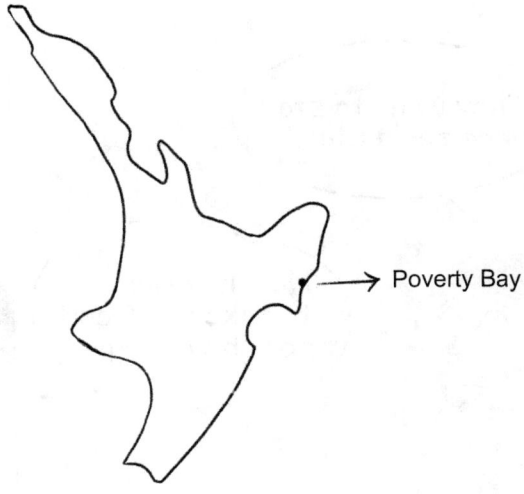

What have been communicated between Tupaia, and the Māori is lost to history, but it probably went something like this: (Disclaimer: This is 100% the writer's speculation.)

With this logic, I don't blame the Māori's hostile reaction.

Back in the ship, Cook must have thought:

Cook's voyage continued, and he pretty much named places - *Oppa British Style* - however he liked, since no one around spoke English anyway.

His other interactions with local people were much friendlier, mostly just gift exchanges.

Cook handed out plenty of British coins, probably hoping that when other Europeans (or anyone else really) showed up later, they'd take one look and think, 'Ah, the British were here first'.

He also decided to plant a British flag, just in case there was any confusion about who visited the land first.

The Māori didn't have a concept about national flags and didn't understand the Brits actions.

To the Māori, it was just a weird piece of fabric stuck in the ground by a bunch of overdressed, pale strangers who clearly hadn't gotten enough sun in a while.

On their way back to the ship, Cook and his crew stumbled across a group of Māori having a meal.

So far, so normal… until they got a little closer.

That's when they noticed something unsettling.

They saw human bones scattered around the campfire.

Cook turned to Tupaia and asked him to find out what was going on.

So, Tupaia went over and asked the Māori about the human bones.

It turns out, the Māori had a custom of eating their defeated enemies, which absolutely shocked the British soldiers.

For the crew, this was a massive blow. Word of what they'd seen spread fast, and soon everyone on the ship was terrified.

As captain, James Cook had to stay cool, calm and display strength.

Let's be real: he was probably freaking out on the inside.

After all, hearing about people eating humans is kind of like hearing someone ate a dog. Disturbing, isn't it?

The *Endeavour* eventually left New Zealand, and Cook named the place Queen Charlotte Sound, AKA Cannibal Bay.

Meanwhile, Banks and Solander had a great time in New Zealand, much like they did back in Tahiti.

While everyone else was stressing about cannibals, they were off on botanical adventures, collecting all sorts of plant samples.

For them, it was all about discovering cool new species!

New Holland

After sailing west from New Zealand, the *Endeavour* finally spotted land. And they saw people on the beach.

Cook recorded the scene in his journal, in which he described a woman and her children:

'They were black or very dark brown, and naked, not even a loin cloth.'

Lucky for Cook, he wasn't around in modern society, otherwise, he'd be roasted online in seconds.

When the locals spotted the *Endeavour* approaching, more men popped out of the bush, probably thinking, 'What is this big thing rising out of the ocean?'

They quickly ushered the women and children back into the bush, leaving just two men standing their ground with spears in hand.

By now, James Cook was feeling pretty confident when it came to handling new encounters.

After all, he'd already dealt with some pretty wild situations — from the unpredictable days in Tahiti, to the tense encounters in New Zealand, and even stumbling across the remains of a cannibal feast.

So, when a couple of locals showed up with spears?

Cook wasn't fazed. He was ready to deal.

Unlike the Tahitians and the Māori, who were fascinated about shiny metal objects, the Aboriginal men weren't impressed at all.

British fired at the men, injuring one of them.

The Aboriginal men escaped.

Seeing what happened, more men emerged from the bush and hurled spears at the intruders in response.

But sadly, their wooden weapons were no match for British muskets.

The loud gunfire and injury sent the group scattering — they retreated into the bush, scared and outgunned.

Cook's crew then went ashore and explored the area.

They entered the locals' huts and took whatever they liked, leaving behind trinkets in exchange, an act Cook considered 'trade,' though there was no agreement from the Aboriginal people.

This marks the first encounter between the Aboriginal people and the European white folks in 1770.

Cook and his crew hung around the area for about a week, searching for resources to restock their supplies.

The local people kept their distance.

Cook and his crew noticed that Aboriginal people would watch them from afar, often from the woods or across the bay. They abandoned their huts and avoided direct contact (well, who wouldn't?).

And, of course, in classic European explorer fashion, Cook couldn't resist the urge to plant a flag and claim the place for Britain — because clearly, naming things that already had owners was just part of the job description.

Thus, Botany Bay was born!

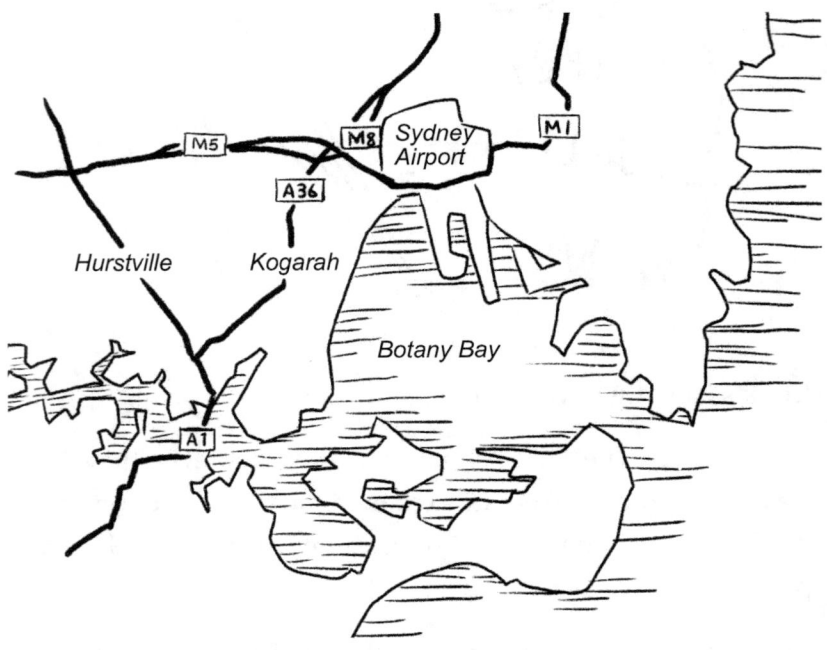

Modern day Botany Bay

James Cook initially wanted to call this bay Stingray Harbour after spotting a bunch of stingrays.

Joseph Banks didn't like the name and suggested another name Botany Bay.

Who knew that this area would eventually turn into today's Sydney Airport? So, next time you're flying into Sydney and the plane's about to land, just remember this is the spot where James Cook first visited Australia in 1770.

Meanwhile, Joseph Banks was living his best life, collecting all sorts of new botanical specimens — plants, animals, insects — you name it.

Cook Town

The Endeavour set sail north, cruising along the Australian east coast. Everything seemed to be going smoothly — new territory mapped, land claimed, mission accomplished. Time to set sail for home!

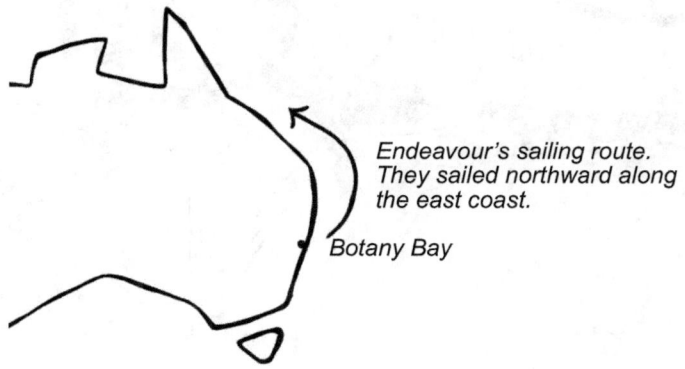

Endeavour's sailing route. They sailed northward along the east coast.
Botany Bay

Then they reached the Great Barrier Reef…

105

Suddenly they bumped the Endeavour onto the coral.

Let's sing along (to the tune of Humpty Dumpty)

🎵 🎵 🎵 🎵
Endeavour sailed along the shore,
Then hit a reef what a roar!
All the Captain's sailors, and all the ship's men,
Couldn't make Endeavour float again.

Everyone feared the worst and they thought the ship would sink. But James Cook, ever the calm leader, sprang into action. He ordered the crew to unload cargo to lighten the ship. Thanks to his quick thinking, disaster was averted.

They somehow managed to get the ship to the nearest land and set up camps to fix the ship.

They ended up staying there for a while.

There is a famous artwork depicting this situation: *The Endeavour, c1770 Engraving by Rennoldson.*

That spot is now called Cooktown. So remember, Cooktown is not where James Cook lived, it's the place where he repaired his ship.

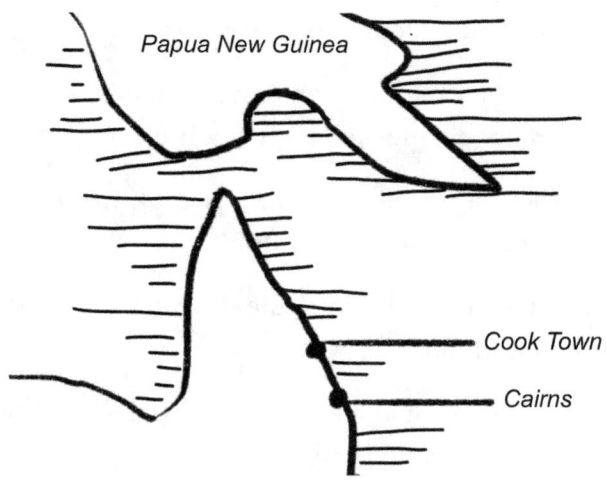

In Cooktown, they stumbled upon a strange-looking creature. Yep, it was their first encounter with a kangaroo!

Joseph Banks was absolutely fascinated when he saw a kangaroo for the first time.

It hopped, it bounced, it looked like nothing he'd ever seen before — part deer, part rabbit, part... box of surprises.

Naturally, he did what any curious gentleman-scientist of the 1700s might do: he grabbed a musket and went hunting.

Banks managed to shoot a couple and proudly took two dead kangaroos back to England as scientific trophies.

One of the skulls even made it into the Royal College of Surgeons' museum in London.

That is... until World War II came along and, well, the skull of kangaroo didn't survive a second time.

Meanwhile, James Cook got busy mapping and claiming the entire east coast of Australia, proudly naming it New South Wales (I guess when it comes to naming sense, he was on par with the Dutch).

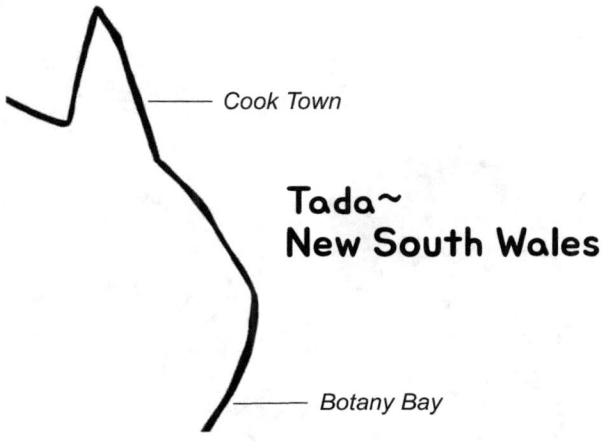

They managed to patch up the Endeavour with whatever materials they could find, just enough to keep it afloat until they reached Jakarta.

Sadly, Tupaia and Taiata didn't make it. They succumbed to disease along the way.

Destroying one of Joseph Banks grand plans to bring them to England to proudly show them to his friends.

Then finally, after nearly three years at sea, countless storms, tropical diseases, ship repairs, and one awkward run-in with cannibals, the Endeavour made it back to England in July 1771.

They returned as heroes.

Cook was praised for his precise mapping and navigation, and Banks became a scientific celebrity.

The kangaroo skull got a front-row seat in a museum.

Not bad for a trip that started with some dots on a star map and a sealed letter marked 'Open later'.

This voyage was a significant mission. Even the King George III took an interest.

Well, not in the whole crew — he was mostly keen to meet Joseph Banks and his scientific sidekick, Dr. Solander.

The two were invited to dine with the King, where they reported their findings about tropical islands, new species and kangaroos.

James Cook was too low-ranking to score an invite to the palace. But he didn't leave empty-handed, he got a promotion to Commander and a very handsome pension.

He embarked on two more voyages during his lifetime and died on his third voyage in Hawaii.

According to legend, he was eaten by the local Hawaiians, but historical accounts suggest he was killed in a conflict (though, I suppose he could have been killed first and then eaten).

His legacy will be remembered forever by Australians, and in the 1930s, his father's cottage (yes, his father's) was shipped all the way to Melbourne and rebuilt.

But *why*, though? I mean, the cottage wasn't even James Cook's house. And Cook had literally nothing to do with Melbourne.

Oh well, who am I to judge?

As for New South Wales?

Neither Cook nor Banks believed that the place was worth conquering or suitable for building a colony. Although Cook claimed sovereignty over the land in the name of the King and raised the Union Jack on the east coast in 1770, the British government took no action for nearly two decades, until 1788.

so far as we know [it] doth not produce any one thing that can became an Article in trade to invite Europeans to fix a settlement upon it.
— James Cook —

CHAPTER 4
The First Fleet

During the reign of King George III, Britain treated their North American colonies like a personal piggy bank — taxing everything that wasn't nailed down.

Eventually, the Americans (well, they weren't 'Americans' yet) snapped. They picked up their muskets and went to war with Britain.

Essentially, it was: King George III vs. George Washington.

One George fought for taxes, the other fought for freedom.

This eight-year war of the 'Battle of the Georges' went down in history as the American Revolution.

America won, kicking Britain's butt.

And just like that, the USA was born — a country of freedom, and a lifelong love of complaining about taxes!

Convicts everywhere

In 18th-century Britain, the First Industrial Revolution boosted productivity like never before, and also created a whole bunch of Convicts.

But how come? Let me explain.

Meet Bob.

He's just a regular British guy, working hard at a cotton mill — nothing fancy, just keeping the cotton flowing and the boss happy.

The cotton merchant needed people like Bob to keep the business running. And it wasn't just cotton — other industries also needed manpower to keep their machines going.

Then — *boom!* — the First Industrial Revolution hit, and machines started doing all of Bob's work (kind of like what AI's doing to us now).

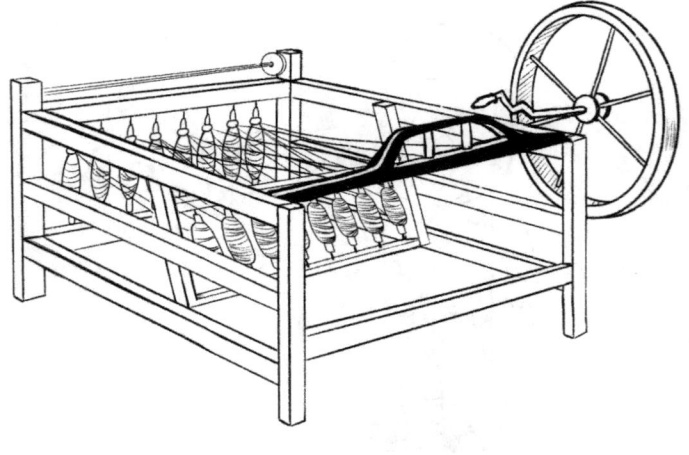

Spinning Jenny

In theory, Bob's productivity boosted — loads of free time, right? (Just like we thought AI would make our lives easier).

Well... not quite.

Before Bob even realised what was happening, machines had taken over the stuff he thought he was still good at, like sweeping up, cleaning toilets, or whatever else he fancied himself useful for. Suddenly, Bob's skills were about as useless as a landline phone.

People like Bob, who couldn't find work, and out of options all moved to the big cities looking for jobs.

Cities became overcrowded, dirty, and full of people with no work and no money.

So, Bob got hungry, he had to steal food for survival.

And – *surprise!* – he got caught and convicted.

Bob went from full-time cotton worker to full-time convict!

18th-century Britain had some *very* creative ideas about crime.

Steal a loaf of bread? — prison.

Look at someone the wrong way? Might as well pack your bags.

Pretend to be a retired soldier? You could get hanged (Yes, cosplaying as a veteran was a life-risking activity).

Caught outdoors after curfew? — Flogged.

Stealing a handkerchief worth more than a shilling, and you could be sentenced to death.

Basically, if you breathed too loudly in the wrong direction, someone in a powdered wig might ship you off to the other side of the world — or straight to meet God.

Suddenly Britain had more convicts than it knew what to do with.

Back in the day, the solution was simple: ship off unwanted people — mainly convicts — to the American colonies.

British judge

But after the American Revolution, America basically said, 'Nope, not our problem anymore.' So now, Britain had a serious problem: too many criminals and nowhere to send them.

Britain needed a new solution. They had to find a new dumping ground for its unwanted criminals (Spoiler: G'day New South Wales).

In the meantime, the British government got creative.

They stuck convicts onto *Hulks* — no, not the big, green, angry smashing monster — but old, rotting ships left to float in rivers and harbours.

The conditions were awful, mice running around like they owned the place, no toilets, no beds and definitely no baths.

Imagine being stuck on a leaky, smelly ship with just a bunch of cranky convicts and angry seagulls squawking at you.

Just pure misery.

With hygiene basically thrown out the window, everyone started getting sick, and diseases were spreading faster than celebrity gossip on the internet.

The British government realised that if they didn't act soon, they wouldn't just have a convict problem, they'd have a full-blown pandemic.

So, after a whole of debate on where to dump — ahem, *relocate* — the growing convict population, Sir Joseph Banks suggested starting a new colony in New South Wales.

However, 18 years earlier Banks had declared New South Wales unfit for a colony an no-one knows why he changed his mind.

Arthur Phillip

Britain decided to establish New South Wales as a new colony (a penal colony for punishment) and needed to pick the right person for the job.

The new colony needed a competent man for the mission. It had to be a man, women couldn't even own property at the time. (And please... don't ask, 'What is a man?' We're not going there.)

Arthur Phillip was chosen to become the first governor of New South Wales.

So why him?

The British government didn't want to spend much.

Think of it like trying to get rid of an old couch, you don't want to pay the council's disposal fee, so you leave it on the kerb and pretend it's 'free to a good home.'

New South Wales was the kerb, and the convicts were the old furniture. Britain dumped them there and hoped someone — *anyone* — would figure out what to do with them.

The ultimate goal was to make the colony self-sufficient; no financial support, no supply ships, just figure it out and survive. That meant growing their own food, building their own houses, and so on.

Phillip had farming experience and actually knew how to grow food: a crucial skill if the colony was ever going to stand on its own two feet.

Phillip began preparing for the long journey by assembling supply ships and naval escorts, then carefully selecting his officers and crew.

The entire process took seven months.

The new colony also needed people with a variety of skills. Carpenters to build housing, farmers to tend the land, and young healthy workers to handle the labour.

Phillip had to make sure all the essential tasks were covered to get the colony up and running smoothly.

He demanded skilled convicts for the First Fleet.

The British government provided him with a group of people with no productive skill.

Such as:

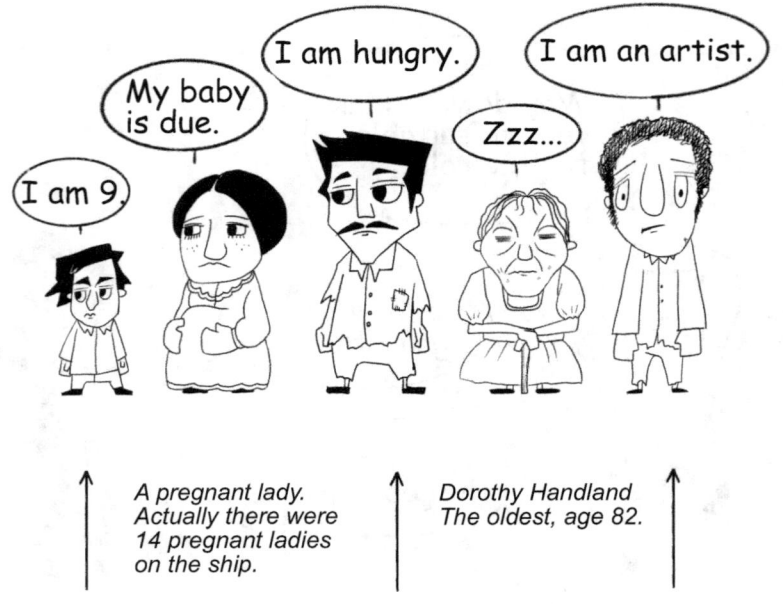

John Hudson.
The youngest convict.

A pregnant lady.
Actually there were
14 pregnant ladies
on the ship.

James Ruse.
Not that famous,
but later he made
contributions in farming
and there is a school
named after him.

Dorothy Handland
The oldest, age 82.

Thomas Barrett.
He will be the first
convict to be hanged.

Phillip had to work with what he was given and embarked on a long voyage.

The First Fleet had 11 ships and 1,500-ish people. About half were sailors and their family members, and the other half were convicts.

What's funny is, there's no single official record of exactly how many convicts were on board. Different documents give different numbers, so the exact figure remains a bit of a mystery. Who knew even the British government could lose track of a few prisoners on a boat?

Arthur Phillip was a man of enlightenment: fair and kind to the convicts. He actually cared about the well-being of the convicts, making sure they had food, basic medical care, and something to wear.

Because many of them showed up half-naked. And Phillip wasn't about to let people roam around the ship with their butts hanging out.

He even let people come out on deck for some fresh air, sunlight, and exercise. A little muscle movement and a dose of Vitamin D — probably the only thing stopping everyone from going crazy after months at sea.

They made three stopovers, loading up on vital farming tools, animals, and crops.

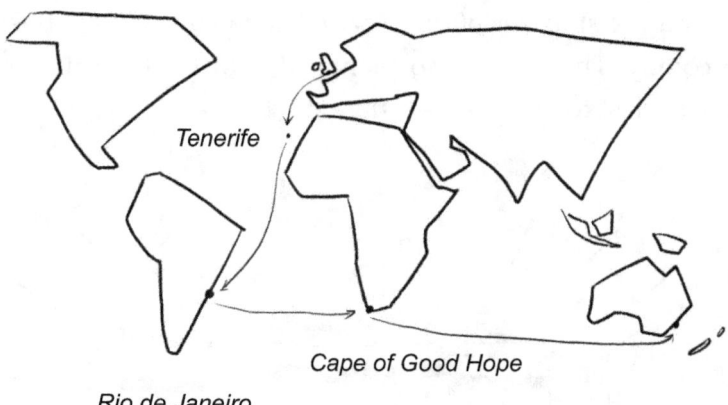

By the end, they had gathered around 500 head of livestock — including cattle, pigs, horses, chickens, goats, and geese.

Although now considered typical of Australia, these animals were all introduced from Europe. None originally belonged to the continent.

Oh, and the ship wasn't just loaded with survival supplies for the colony. There was also plenty of rum for the sailors, and even a priest to oversee the religious services.

Rum wasn't just a treat for rowdy sailors — it was a daily essential in Royal Navy life. In the 18th century, rum rations were considered key to survival.

Fresh water often went stale or became undrinkable during long voyages, but rum didn't spoil. Mixed with water to make 'grog', it made hydration safer — and far more tolerable.

Rum also doubled as a makeshift medicine. It was poured on wounds and used to ease pain. Just as importantly, it kept morale high: feeling seasick, homesick, or just sick of everyone? *Have some rum!*.

Without it, months at sea in cramped, miserable conditions could easily lead to chaos. So yes, rum was just as critical for keeping the whole mission afloat.

Rum was like the *Elixir* from your RPG video game — it healed wounds, boosted morale, and kept the party from falling apart.

They also had unwanted company... the ships were infested with mice.

No, I meant mice!

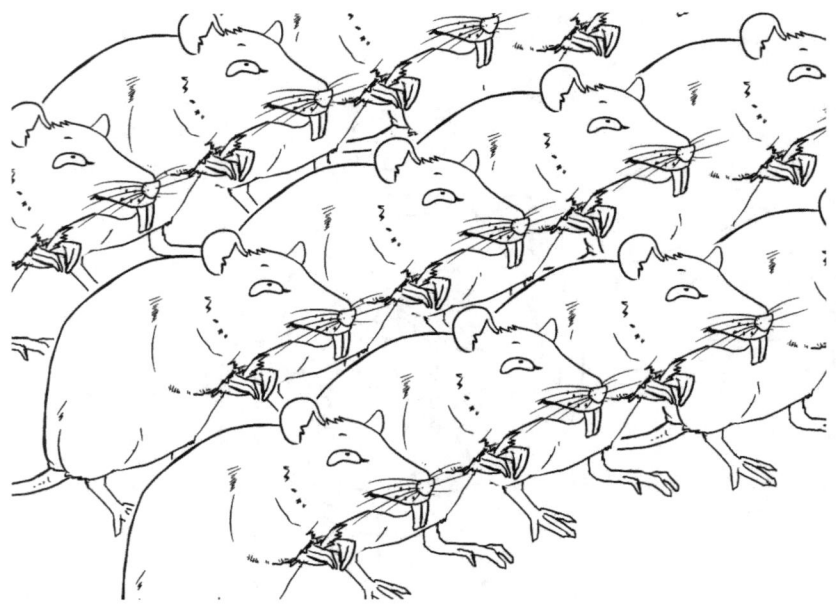

Cockroaches, lice, and bed bugs.

So, yeah, the First Fleet was basically a government-funded circus on water — complete with animals, pests, and a touch of divine intervention.

The white people are here

They made it! After an exhausting eight-month journey, the First Fleet has finally arrived at Botany Bay!

Arthur Phillip landing in New South Wales

Seriously, this is the image you get when you google 'Arthur Phillip'.

And **crap!**

Botany Bay wasn't the best spot for a colony because:

- There wasn't enough fresh drinking water.
- The land was too barren for farming.
- There was no proper shelter for ships.

Phillip quickly decided to explore the northern part of New South Wales and ended up finding a better spot: Port Jackson.

On January 26 in 1788, Phillip named the place Sydney Cove after his boss's name Lord Sydney (First-rate butt-kissing).

Then he planted the British flag and claimed the land in the name of King George III.

This date would later be known as Australia day.

For local Aboriginal people, this meant invasion.

Chapter 5
Tough Times in NSW

Potential famine

When Phillip began settling New South Wales, things got tough fast and one of the biggest problems was food shortage.

Supplies were running low, the soil was dry and unfriendly, and people got hungry *really* quickly.

To stop things from spiralling into full-blown starvation, Phillip acted swiftly. He enforced strict rations and wrote to Britain for more food and supplies.

But desperate people do desperate things: soon, some began stealing from government food stores. To keep order, Phillip had no choice but to introduce harsh punishments, including executions.

The first person hanged in the new colony was Thomas Barrett.

Charlotte Medal *Thomas Barrett*

Barrett was also an artist and crafted the Charlotte Medal, a coin commemorating the First Fleet's arrival. It now lives in the National Maritime Museum.

Who knows? If he had lived, he might have become a famous artist.

While waiting for supplies from Britain, Phillip also sent John Hunter aboard the HMS *Sirius* to the Cape of Good Hope (a Dutch colony at the time) to bring back more supplies.

HMS Sirius

Then Phillip decided to make a new settlement in Norfolk Island.

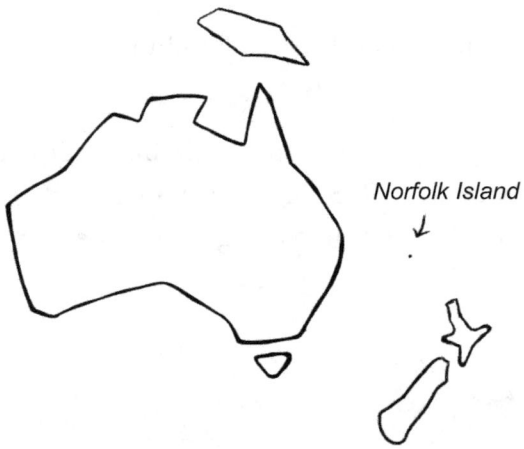

He put Philip Gidley King in charge of this settlement.

The plan was to ease food shortages in the main settlement of New South Wales by sending convicts to the island, hoping they could grow enough surplus crops to help feed the colony.

Oh, Hunter… not again!

While Phillip was struggling to manage the food crisis and anxiously waiting for supply ships from Britain, John Hunter returned with extra supplies from the Cape of Good Hope. But they weren't enough. So, Phillip sent him on another important mission — to sail to China to buy more food and supplies.

This time, Phillip also ordered Hunter to drop off some extra convicts at Norfolk Island along the way, to ease the pressure on New South Wales.

But John Hunter had a special skill when it came to ships.

Just as the Sirius approached Norfolk Island, fully loaded with people and provisions, it shipwrecked.

There is always *that* guy in a team, eh?

Philip Gidley King, already on the island, watched the whole thing unfold — and with it, watched the supplies sink into uselessness.

Luckily no one died in the wreck, but the supplies were spoiled. There just wasn't enough food to go around in Norfolk Island, and things were looking bleak.

Just then, a flock of birds showed up. As though a gift from the heavens.

King ordered his crew to shoot the birds for food.

The bird known as the Norfolk Island pigeon was large, gentle, and completely unafraid of humans. It would perch quietly in the trees, eyeing people with a kind of innocent curiosity, completely unaware of the danger it was in.

With no instinct to flee and nowhere to hide, it quickly became a favourite target for settlers desperate for fresh meat.

One officer even remarked that you could catch them, 'with the hand or a stick', they were that easy to catch.

Thanks to the pigeons a catastrophe was avoided, but as a consequence the species was hunted to extinction not long after.

Back in New South Wales, Governor Phillip was furious when he heard about the *Sirius* shipwreck — and for good reason.

The HMS *Sirius* was the most important ship in the First Fleet: the only real battleship, the fastest vessel, and the colony's main form of transport and defence all in one.

Losing it was a major blow, jus like the moment the Titanic sunk.

Phillip later sent John Hunter back to England to face a court-martial.

The Second Fleet

The food shortage Phillip faced was solved by the extra food and supplies brought by the Second Fleet.

But the Second Fleet had a terrible reputation. One of its ships was called the 'Hell Ship'.

The conditions on board were horrific: convicts had no exercise time, they were poorly fed, and the cells were so overcrowded that they couldn't lie down to sleep.

Many convicts didn't survive the voyage, and about half of the survivors were in critical condition when they finally reached the shores of New South Wales.

The Second Fleet

Phillip was furious about the mistreatment and the conditions on the Second Fleet, so he filed an official complaint to Britain.

But what went wrong?

The First Fleet had been funded by the Crown, using the King's own money — but it turned out to be way too expensive.

So, for the Second Fleet, the British government decided to outsource the job to private companies to cut costs.

It's kind of like what phone companies do today — outsourcing their customer service to India.

These companies were paid based on how many convicts they could ship out of Britain, not how many actually survived the journey to Sydney.

This led shipowners to prioritise quantity over quality, cramming as many convicts onboard as possible with little concern for their condition.

As a result, the Second Fleet became one of the worst voyages in convict history.

Relationship with Aboriginal people

When Phillip arrived in NSW, he had a direct order from Britain to be friendly and find a way to coexist with the land's native people.

So, he decided to offer some gifts to the Aboriginal people. These were mostly everyday items from England, like fabrics, mirrors, beads, and shiny metal bits that sparkled in the sun.

But what he didn't know was that the germs they brought with them were incredibly deadly to the Aboriginals.

It led to a smallpox outbreak that wiped out most of the local population.

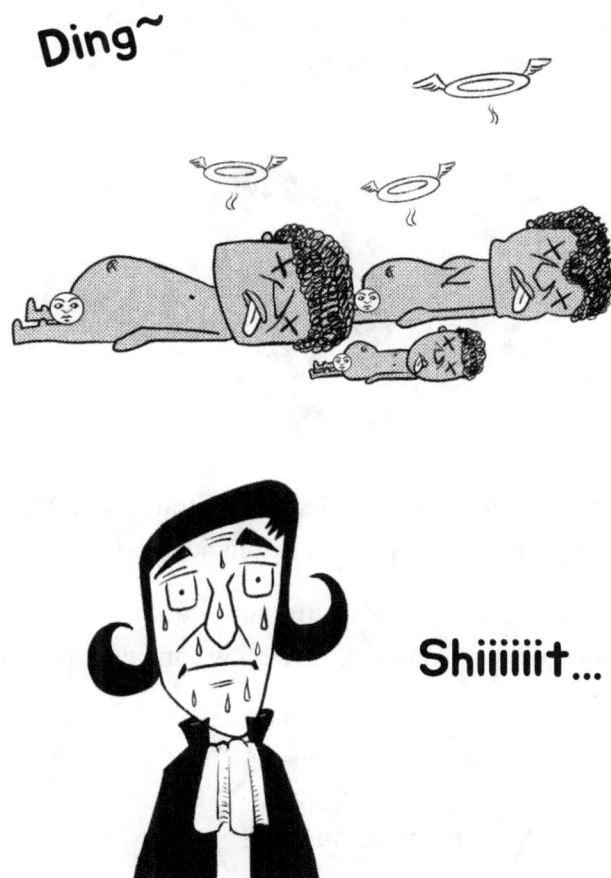

The thing is, there was a smallpox virus bottle on board the First Fleet, meant for experiments.

It turned out the bottle had broken, and the virus spread throughout the colony, killing many Aboriginal people.

The weird part? No one really knew how the virus got out or who was responsible.

Bennelong

Phillip also tried to connect with the Aboriginal people, hoping to find someone who could act as an ambassador between the British and the local communities.

He came up with a great idea — Kidnapping. Yep, I know, kidnapping is the best way to establish friendship, isn't it?

He sent out his men to capture some aboriginal people, and they managed to grab two, one of whom was a man named Bennelong.

Portrait of Bennelong created while he was in England.

Phillip kept them for a while, hoping to prove that the British didn't mean them any harm (You know, apart from the whole kidnapping thing).

One of the men escaped, but Bennelong stuck around for a while. During his stay, Bennelong learned English manners, tried their food, and grew fond of wine and rum. He even wore British clothing now and then.

Over time, he and Phillip developed something that vaguely resembled a friendship.

That is, until Bennelong quietly left the British camp without saying a word.

Sometime later, while Phillip and his men were walking along the beach, they spotted Bennelong with a group of Aboriginal people feasting on a stranded whale.

Bennelong saw Phillip and invited him to join the feast.

But as Phillip approached, suddenly one of the men threw a spear, striking him in the shoulder.

Phillip was quickly taken back to the British camp by his troops, and thankfully, he survived.

To everyone's surprise, Bennelong visited him several times afterward, genuinely concerned for his well-being.

Phillip, in turn, chose not to seek revenge, hoping to maintain peace.

No one knows exactly why Phillip got speared, but historians reckon it was payback for the time the British kidnapped Bennelong and his mate. From the Aboriginal point of view, the spearing could have been a way of restoring balance or honour.

After the incident, their friendly relationship continued. Phillip even gave Bennelong a cottage, which came to be known as *Bennelong's Point*. Today, that very spot is home to Australia's most iconic building: the Sydney Opera House.

Sydney Opera House AKA Bennelong's Point.

But unlike Bennelong, most other Aboriginals were resisting the white people's invasion and their growing presence. One of the most famous being Pemulwuy.

Pemulwuy

Pemulwuy was a local warrior who wasn't happy about white settlers taking his land.

He soon became known for fiercely resisting British expansion, leading attacks to defend his people and territory.

He had a noticeable blemish or speck in one of his eyes, and one of his feet was *clubbed* — it was deformed or abnormally shaped.

Pemulwuy really upset Phillip when he killed Phillip's gamekeeper. John McIntyre (basically the guy in charge of hunting, not a gamer who's good at the Nintendo Switch).

One day, McIntyre spotted Pemulwuy — and from the look they gave each other, it wasn't their first meeting. Then, without warning, Pemulwuy hurled a spear straight into McIntyre's lung. He was dragged back to the settlement, but a few days later, he was dead.

Phillip was determined to capture Pemulwuy, but after years of 'Catch me if you can', he never managed to avenge his gamekeeper before his time in charge was up.

Arthur Phillip left New South Wales in 1792 after five years as governor, because of his declining health.

Arthur Phillip may not have been flashy, but he laid the foundation for the colony's survival. He kept order, made sure people were fed (mostly), and tried to treat both convicts and Aboriginal people with some basic decency — which was rare for the time. Quietly and steadily, he set the tone for what the colony could become.

Bennelong was invited to England by Arthur Phillip, becoming the first Aboriginal person to travel there.

He spent three years abroad before returning to Australia. Eventually, he rejoined his own tribe — but sadly, in his later years, he became an alcoholic and died in 1813.

Meanwhile, Pemulwuy led a series of raids against British settlements.

He and his followers employed guerrilla tactics, hitting settlers and soldiers alike in surprise attacks.

His knowledge of the land, his leadership, and his ability to elude capture made him a feared figure.

Pemulwuy kept up the fight until 1802, when he was finally shot dead.

The British preserved his head in some mystery liquid — like a pickled cucumber — and shipped it off to Joseph Banks for 'scientific study'.

CHAPTER 6
Hunter VS Macarthur

After Phillip left, New South Wales was left without a governor because the British government was too caught up dealing with the chaos of the French Revolution.

France was busy chopping off heads, including that of their own king, Louis XVI and this wild new idea of democracy started spreading to Britain.

King George III got worried that he might end up like Louis XVI. So no-one gave any attention to a small, distant penal colony full of rum and convicts.

It ended up taking the British government three years to officially appoint a new governor for New South Wales.

Phillip suggested Philip Gildley King to be his successor.

They ignored Phillip's advice entirely and sent John Hunter instead (Yes, the same guy who wrecked the *HMS Sirius*).

When Hunter finally arrived in Sydney in 1795, the colony was in complete chaos — corruption was rampant, and drunkenness seemed to be everywhere.

So, what happened during those three years?

Back then Sydney didn't have currency, so people had to rely on bartering. That is, trading goods for other goods.

But bartering wasn't easy. It was hard to find the perfect match — like when both people actually wanted what the other had.

But one thing was wildly popular and nearly everyone was happy to trade for it:

Alcohol!

The British navy had a tradition of drinking rum. it was strong, cheap to produce and easy to supply in bulk.

So naturally rum quickly became the unofficial currency for New South Wales.

But who was in control of the rum?

The Marines and the New South Wales Corps.

As we mentioned earlier, the First Fleet didn't just bring convicts, it also brought Marines and their families.

They were hoping for a better life and fresh opportunities in the new land, only to find the soil barren and harsh living conditions. It didn't even offer real money.

With rum becoming the 'money' of the colony, the Marines and the New South Wales Corps saw a golden opportunity. They were the only ones who could buy rum in large amounts from passing ships, effectively giving them full control over the supply.

They quickly monopolised the rum trade, using it to maximise their own profits by trading it for goods, labour, and service, running the colony like a private business, with rum as their personal ATM.

Therefore, the New South Wales Corps was also known as the *Rum Corps*.

Ever wondered if people made their own spirits?

Well, they tried.

But whenever someone set up a private still to produce booze, guess what happened?

They got shut down. *Fast.*

Because just like how you can't print your own money today, you couldn't make your own rum back then.

If you or I tried to print money now, it'd be called counterfeiting — and we'd be in serious legal trouble. We're only allowed to use money issued by official authorities.

Anyone who tried to make their own rum would be beaten up by the Rum Corps and their rum taken away.

In the absence of a governor, the colony was left in the hands of Major Francis Grose, head of the New South Wales Corps — a man very open to bribery and flattery.

He abolished many of Phillip's fair policies, especially the one about giving equal food rations to convicts and soldiers.

Instead, he started rewarding officers with land grants, convict labour, and rum.

Basically turning the colony into a military-run business.

One of his favourites was John Macarthur.

John Macarthur

John Macarthur arrived in the colony as part of the New South Wales corps on the Second Fleet.

He was in it for power, land, and profit. The kind of guy you'd expect to see in an old TV show; the greedy boss who's always demanding *more* and never satisfied with what he's already got.

He was a pro at kissing up to Major Francis Grose, and quickly became one of his favourites in the corps.

Thanks to that, he was given a massive chunk of land, a free workforce of convicts, and control over the colony's rum trade, which was as good as printing his own money.

The combination of Major Grose's corrupted leadership and Macarthur's profit-hungry ambition gave the Rum Corps free reign to exploit the colony.

They charged sky-high prices and used rum to control trade, labour, and convicts — all for their own gain.

Some records even show that people worked for days just to earn a single bottle of rum.

People loved drinking and rum had basically become money. So why not just let them be? What is the problem, why all the fuss?

Well, excessive drinking comes with two major problems:

Unproductivity and social chaos.

Let's put it this way.

Imagine your dad — normally a hardworking, responsible guy.

But one day, he starts drinking like there is no tomorrow.

Then,

- His boss gets frustrated because he's no longer productive, so he gets fired.
- Your mum is upset because there's no income to support the family.

- Feeling hopeless, he might even turn to crime, stealing or robbing just to get by.

Now, imagine this happening not just in your house, but across the whole society. Productivity crashes and crime skyrockets.

That's exactly what was happening in New South Wales when Governor Hunter returned.

Society was spiralling out of control, and something had to be done.

Hunter's plan and the big problem

Governor Hunter had two major plans:

- Restrict Rum Imports — Less alcohol available meant fewer drunk people, which (in theory) should have led to a more stable society.

- Encourage Farming — If people grew their own food, they would rely less on imported goods, including rum.

Sounds like a solid plan, right? Here is the catch:

Any policy, or plan, needs enforcement.

Someone to make sure people follow the rules, and that's usually the job of the military or police.

The irony was the very people who were supposed to enforce Hunter's rum restrictions were the same people making the most money from the rum trade.

At the heart of all this? John Macarthur.

He wasn't just involved in the rum trade — he was running the show.

Macarthur persuaded the soldiers to ignore Hunter's orders.

And since the soldiers were already profiting from the trade, they were more than happy to listen to Macarthur instead.

In other words, Hunter wasn't just fighting against the rum trade, he was up against an entire system built on corruption, with Macarthur right at the centre.

So, surprise, surprise, Hunter's reforms weren't exactly popular.

The Corps, already knee-deep in corruption, had no interest in shutting down their most profitable business.

Instead of enforcing the restrictions, they actively worked against them, making sure the rum kept flowing and the profits kept coming.

After all, when nearly everyone in the military is making money from the rum trade, and then one guy suddenly tries to shut it down... Well, you can imagine how that went.

Hunter reported the corruption to Britain, especially naming Macarthur and the New South Wales Corps. He hoped the government would step in with strict intervention.

Macarthur fought back by sending his own reports back to Britain. According to him, it wasn't the rum trade or corruption causing social chaos, it was Hunter's incompetence and his mismanagement that had turned New South Wales into a colony of drunkards and criminals.

In the end, the British government believed Macarthur and recalled Hunter in 1800.

Macarthur had won the first round against the governors of New South Wales.

Reporting back to Britain!

Reporting back to Britain too!

Although John Hunter wasn't the most successful governor, he played a key role in supporting exploration — especially during the time when two of the colony's most famous explorers, Matthew Flinders and George Bass, made groundbreaking discoveries under his watch.

The two close friends set out in a tiny boat and proved that Van Diemen's Land (now Tasmania) was not part of the mainland, but a separate island.

In 1798, they named the body of water between the island and the continent Bass Strait, after George Bass himself.

The relationship between Matthew Flinders and George Bass remains a mystery today.

They named the ocean strait, but were they straight?

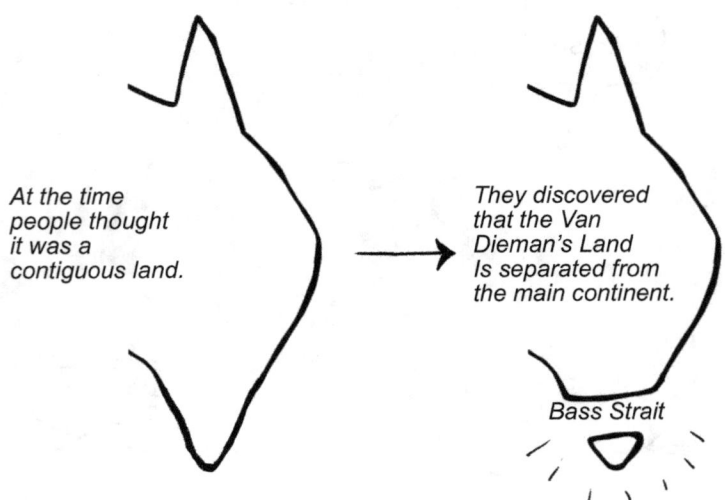

CHAPTER 7
King VS Macarthur

Philip Gidley King succeeded John Hunter and became the third governor of NSW in 1800 — someone finally took Arthur Phillip's advice.

King believed Hunter had been too weak to control the corrupt New South Wales Corps. He was determined to restore order to the colony.

King was believed to be more competent and assertive than Hunter, and during his time as governor several historical events unfolded.

He followed his predecessor's policy and backed Flinders in completing the coastal map of Australia.

In 1803, Matthew Flinders achieved the first circumnavigation of Australia, confirming that New South Wales was part of a single landmass, not broken up by sea.

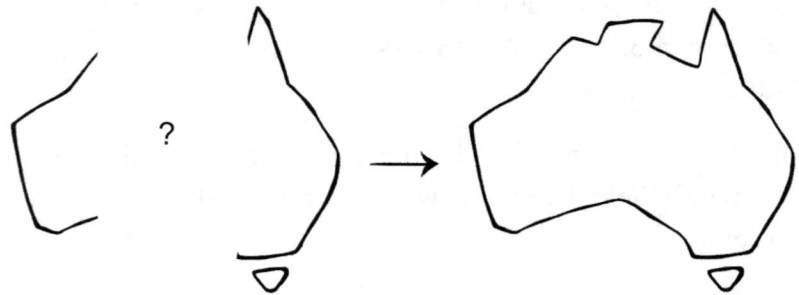

Before Matthew Flinders, people weren't even sure if Australia was one big landmass.

Many thought New South Wales was divided by ocean into two separate places.

But Flinders proved there wasn't sea in between; it was a contiguous continent.

Sadly, that same year his close friend George Bass went missing at sea and was never seen again.

Shortly after, Flinders was imprisoned by the French on the island of Mauritius, a French colony, and held for seven years.

In 1814, he wrote a book in which he used the term 'Australia' to refer to New South Wales.

The name was later picked up by Governor Lachlan Macquarie, who suggested it be adopted officially — and in 1824, it became the official name of the colony.

New settlement in Van Diemen's Land

While Flinders was circumnavigating Australia, French ships led by Nicolas Baudin were also doing the same.

Baudin spent a long time in Van Diemen's Land (Tasmania), collecting local species and interacting with the Indigenous people.

This made Governor King nervous — what if the French claimed Van Diemen's Land for themselves? To prevent that, in 1803 he sent Lieutenant John Bowen to establish a presence on the island.

At the same time, King ordered David Collins to set up a new settlement at Port Phillip (modern-day Melbourne).

The idea was that if the French tried to claim Van Diemen's Land, Collins' colony could support Bowen's settlement.

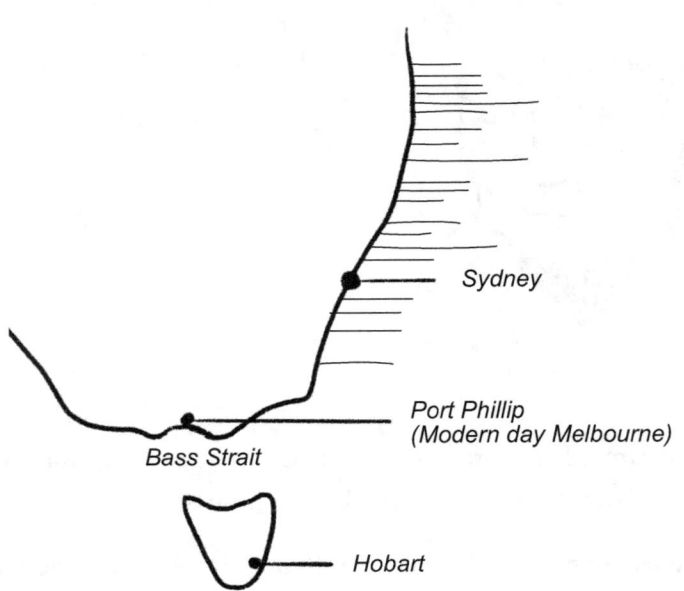

In an attempt to settle Port Phillip, Collins brought around 370 people — most of them convicts. Among them was William Buckley.

But things didn't go as planned. The soil was too sandy for farming, the timber quality was too poor, and the local people were too hostile.

Collins quickly realised the settlement wasn't sustainable and abandoned Port Phillip.

He decided to relocate everyone to Van Diemen's Land. William Buckley saw his chance. Grabbing a kettle (I don't know why a kettle), he escaped into the wilderness, vanishing into the unknown.

Collins moved to Hobart with help from John Bowen, and together they began settling Van Diemen's Land.

But their new colony wasn't just about farms and tents, it came with drama too. Both David Collins and John Bowen had mistresses during their time in the colony.

Collins, despite having a wife back in England, started a relationship with Margaret Eddington, a 16-year-old female convict. They went on to have two children together.

Bowen followed a similar path: he also took a mistress and had two children with her. But unlike Collins, Bowen later abandoned his new family and returned to Britain, leaving them behind.

The Castle Hill Rebellion

This was an uprising led by a group of Irish political convicts who wanted to overthrow British rule in New South Wales — and somehow, someday, find their way back to Ireland.

Here's a bit of background:

Back in 1798, a group called the Society of United Irishmen staged a rebellion against British rule in Ireland. The British crushed the rebellion, and many of its leaders — including Philip Cunningham — who were captured and sentenced to exile.

'Death or liberty!' was my catch phrase!

Ironically, instead of sending them to different parts of the world, the British government sent a bunch of them to the same place: New South Wales.

Because, apparently, putting all your political enemies in one colony was a *great* idea.

Cunningham reunited with his former rebel mates, and their ambition to take control was reignited.

On the night of March 4th 1804, Philip Cunningham gathered around 220 Irish convicts from the Castle Hill work camp and launched their long-awaited rebellion.

They attacked a nearby government farm, seized weapons, and then split into smaller groups to raid surrounding farmhouses.

However, many of them got lost in the dark (turns out, their worst enemy wasn't the British — it was darkness!).

The British authorities quickly caught wind of the rebellion when one of the rebels, frightened, decided to reveal their plan.

Governor Philip Gidley King acted fast.

He declared martial law, giving the New South Wales Corps the authority to shoot rebels on sight, and appointed Major George Johnston in charge of crushing the uprising.

You can't talk about Australian rebellions without mentioning the Johnstons.

I shut one down... my nephew helped spark one.

Rebellion runs in the family.

Johnston rolled up to the Castle Hill showdown with just 60 men: not exactly an army, more like a tough-looking rugby team. When it came time to face off against the rebels, he figured a chat might go further than a charge.

Grabbing a white flag, he strolled into the middle of the field and invited the rebel leaders to talk it out.

Out came Phillip Cunningham and another senior rebel, William Johnston (no relation to George, yeah... the names are confusing).

While they were deep in discussion, George pulled a quick move — like something out of a *John Wick* action movie — and captured both leaders on the spot.

Then, without missing a beat, he gave the order for his troops to attack the now-leaderless rebels.

The British troops opened fire at the rebels.

In no time, about 15 rebels were killed and many others fled into the bush.

The uprising was crushed.

Cunningham and Johnston, along with seven other rebel leaders were hanged.

The dance of the hanged man x 9

Although the rebellion failed, it remains a powerful symbol of convict resistance and the growing discontent with British rule. It was an early fight against oppression and inequality — a bold, if doomed, stand for freedom.

Almost 50 years later, another Irish-influenced rebellion would shake the colony, this time at the Eureka Stockade.

But unlike Castle Hill, that one actually left a mark, helping to steer Australia toward major political reforms and a more democratic future.

King's bitter war against John Macarthur

By this time, John Macarthur had become incredibly influential, having made his fortune by importing the first Merino sheep from the Cape of Good Hope.

Thanks to Australia's climate, the sheep's fine wool flourished, and Macarthur quickly became known as the pioneer of the Australian wool industry.

Governor King, like Hunter before him, tried to enforce fair policies and reign in the power of the New South Wales Corps, but Macarthur, as always, opposed just about everything King tried to implement.

By this point, King had realised just how impossible it was to deal with the insubordinate Corps. Then suddenly, one incident gave him the perfect chance to strike back.

Macarthur, known for being outspoken, ambitious, and constantly argumentative, clashed with Colonel William Paterson, the acting commander of the Corps (which meant he was Macarthur's boss).

Their heated dispute escalated into a duel, where Macarthur shot and wounded Paterson — a serious offence.

King saw this as an opportunity to remove Macarthur.

He had him arrested and sent back to England for trial, hoping this would finally end his influence in New South Wales.

However, Macarthur used his political connections in London to defend himself and spread further criticism of King's leadership.

The charges against him were dropped. Instead of being punished, Macarthur was rewarded for an even larger area of land in New South Wales. Strengthening his empire even further.

Macarthur and the Rum Corps kept sending negative reports about King to Britain, painting him as ineffective. It worked, King resigned in 1806.

King was an interesting character. While he was overseeing Norfolk Island, he took a female convict named Anna as his mistress and had two sons with her.

He named them Norfolk and Sydney (after the two colonies).

Later, he went back to England and married his cousin Ann, whose name was strikingly similar to his mistress's (Makes you wonder if he had a thing for names starting with 'An').

Unlike many officers of his time, he *didn't* abandon his children. Instead, he took them back to England, made sure they got a proper education, and even paved the way for their careers in the Royal Navy.

Oh! I can't forget to mention this little twist: while King was cracking down on drinking in the colony, he was reportedly a heavy drinker himself.

CHAPTER 8
Legendary Bligh

Macarthur's biggest battle and greatest triumph would come when he went up against the fourth governor, William Bligh.

Bligh was once a rising star in the British Royal Navy.

He'd been hand-picked by none other than James Cook for Cook's third voyage, and he was present when Cook was killed in Hawaii.

After that, Bligh steadily climbed the naval ranks, building a reputation for being skilled, bold, and a little hot-headed.

Later, Joseph Banks gave him a special mission.

He was ordered to sail to Tahiti and collect breadfruit (a tropical fruit about the size of a small soccer ball) to be used as a cheap food source for slaves.

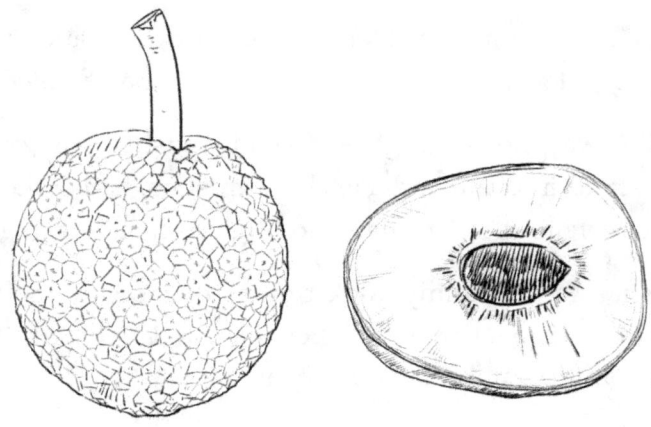

Breadfruit

Bligh was made captain of the HMS *Bounty* for this mission, and that's where his legend really began.

He was a highly competent man, great at navigation, skilled in cartography (map making) and known for his discipline.

But there was one big problem.

Bligh had a serious temper.

He'd get angry easily and wasn't shy about blasting foul language — lots of F-words (F is not for *fish* for sure) which kept his crew constantly on edge.

Like I mentioned earlier in the book, Tahiti was like paradise for these young, stressed-out sailors.

They'd spent most of their lives at sea, doing tough daily chores, so the abundant food and romantic attention from local women must've seemed like a dream come true.

The crew pretty much had zero interest in leaving Tahiti.

When it came time to sail back to cold, grey England with Bligh barking orders nonstop, the crew was less than thrilled.

On the way home, Bligh eventually pushed things too far. His second-in-command, Fletcher Christian, had enough of the constant yelling, strict rules, and Bligh being a total nightmare.

Christian led a mutiny, took control of the ship, and kicked Bligh and 18 loyal crew members off the *Bounty*, leaving them with nothing but a small open boat.

Out you go!

Armed with just basic supplies and a sextant (no compass!) Bligh navigated over 6,700 kilometres of open ocean, from Tofua to Batavia (modern-day Timor) using nothing but the stars.

They were at sea for 47 days and Bligh kept nearly all his men alive.

Only one crew member was lost. Killed and eaten by locals on the island of Tofua, during a brief stop for supplies.

The mutiny became so famous that it's still talked about today.

It inspired countless books and movies, including the 1984 Hollywood film *The Bounty,* starring Mel Gibson as Fletcher Christian and Anthony Hopkins as Bligh.

Because of that, William Bligh became the most well-known Australian governor known to a worldwide audience.

After King, the British government finally recognised how serious the Rum Corps problem had become, and they wanted someone who could enforce strict discipline.

Once again, Joseph Banks recommended William Bligh for the job.

Bligh decided to bring his daughter Mary and her husband with him to Sydney, because his own wife thought New South Wales was a terrible place to be and the journey was too long. So, she stayed behind.

By the time Bligh arrived in Sydney, Macarthur had grown even more powerful and influential.

The two strong-willed men clashed hard right from the start.

Bligh went full force against the rum trade — determined to rip it out of the colony's economy.

The rum trade system in New South Wales worked like this:

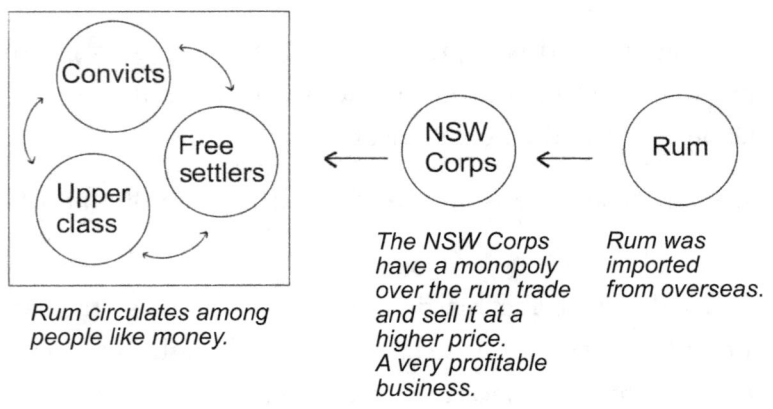

Rum circulates among people like money.

The NSW Corps have a monopoly over the rum trade and sell it at a higher price. A very profitable business.

Rum was imported from overseas.

Bligh's first move was to break the system by taking over the importing process.

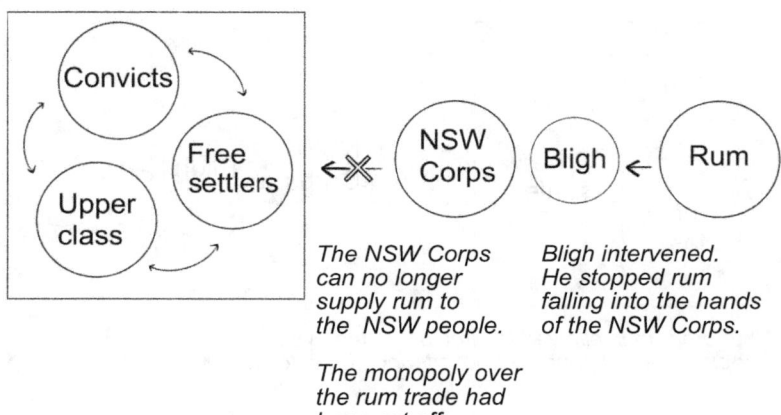

This intervention would end the monopoly of the NSW Corps on rum, upsetting many of those making profits, especially John Macarthur.

Bligh then banned the use of rum as currency altogether, but he didn't introduce a replacement system.

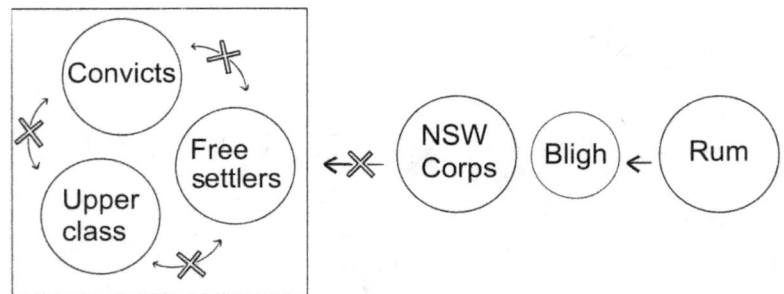

No more rum is allowed to circulate in the system. People were left confused, wondering, 'how do we buy stuff?'.

To make things worse (or better, depending on your perspective), Bligh started removing wealthy and powerful people from key administrative roles: firing people Elon Musk-style, clearing house like it was Twitter HQ.

His final step was to confiscate any privately stored rum. In modern terms, that's like the government taking all the money out of your saving account.

Imagine this.

Bob had been doing well in New South Wales. He was working hard, earning money, got himself a promotion and even had some savings (a respectable boxful of rum stashed at home).

Then, out of nowhere, the government drops a bombshell: 'Your money (rum) is no longer valid'.

Confused, Bob asks, 'Okay... so what's the replacement?'. They just shrug and say, 'We don't have one'.

Before he can even process it, he loses his job. No warning, no backup plan. Just — *poof* — gone.

Bob thinks, 'Well, at least I've got my savings to fall back on'.

Guess what? The government swoops in and takes that too.

Of course this iron-fisted style made people like Bob upset.

Turns out Bligh had a real talent for making enemies: not just Macarthur's supporters, but also people who didn't even like Macarthur.

Frustrated and fed up with Bligh, people put their differences aside and joined forces.

It was the classic 'my enemy's enemy is my friend' situation. Except this time, it was the whole colony against one man.

After all, nothing unites people quite like a common enemy. And Bligh? He fit the role perfectly.

The tension finally reached a breaking point, and the sparks that would ignite the Rum Rebellion began to fly.

The Rum Rebellion

The fuse was lit when a convict escaped the colony by hiding aboard one of Macarthur's ships.

Bligh, seeing this as a clear violation of the law, sought to hold Macarthur accountable and fined him.

Macarthur, of course, refused to pay.

In response, Bligh asked the Judge Advocate Richard Atkins to summon Macarthur to court.

But Macarthur, in true Macarthur fashion, refused to appear. Arguing that Atkins had previously borrowed money from him and was therefore not qualified to act as a judge in his case.

Bligh, now furious, took matters into his own hands and ordered Macarthur's arrest.

But thanks to his powerful connections, Macarthur was quickly released on bail.

When Macarthur finally appeared at the court, he launched a blistering attack on Richard Atkins, mocking his character, debt, and incompetence.

His words, sharp and filled with venom, echoed through the courtroom, and it became clear that he had no respect for the legal system — or Bligh's authority.

The six magistrates present, all of them friends and allies of Macarthur, sided with him.

Together, Macarthur and the magistrates undermined Atkins so thoroughly that Atkins, unable to bear the pressure, eventually fled away from the courthouse.

The trial couldn't go ahead. Without a judge advocate to lead the proceedings the whole thing fell apart in embarrassing fashion.

Bligh was furious (though he seems to be angry all the time).

To him, this was more than just a failed trial. It was an act of defiance that bordered on treason.

Mad as a cut snake, he ordered Major George Johnston to arrest Macarthur, and the six magistrates involved.

Arrest them all!

However, Johnston, claimed he was unable to carry out Bligh's orders due to his injury from couple of days earlier.

In a twist of fate, that very night, Johnston seeing an opportunity, went to see MacArthur instead.

The two men quickly hatched a plan. They organised a petition with over 150 signatures, calling for the removal of Governor Bligh.

On January 26th, 1808, exactly 20 years after the First Fleet arrived, about 400 soldiers, led by Major George Johnston, marched toward Government House to arrest Governor Bligh.

They stormed the building, sending servants fleeing and furniture crashing as they forced their way inside.

But one person refused to back down — Mary Bligh.

As the soldiers burst into Government House, Mary Bligh stood her ground — armed with nothing but her parasol.

She swung it fiercely, refusing to back down.

But it wasn't enough, the soldiers seized Governor Bligh, dragging him from his hiding place.

Some say he was hiding under a bed: a final, humiliating moment that would haunt his legacy forever.

His time as governor ended after just 18 months.

For John Macarthur, this marks the ultimate victory! Three governors challenged, and three governors down, achieving a 'triple kill'.

**Import ban.
Heavy fine.
Arresting for trial.**

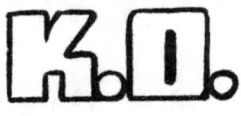
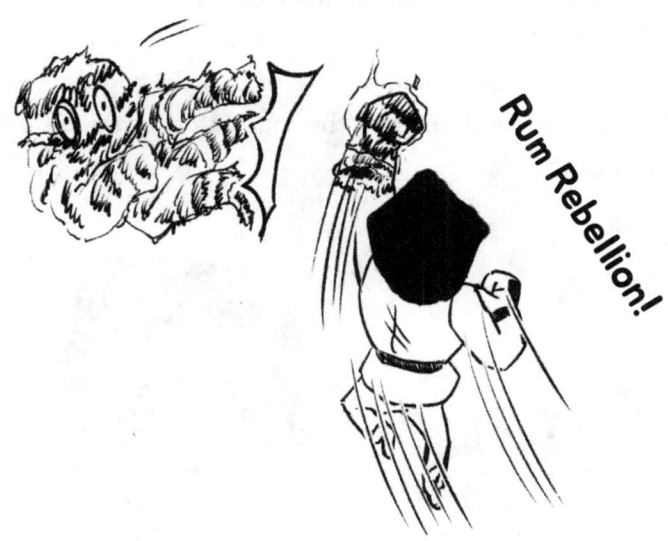

CHAPTER 9
The Father of Australia

After Bligh's downfall, the British government sought a new kind of leader. Instead of another Marine, they appointed a military man Lachlan Macquarie as the fifth governor of New South Wales: he will become the man later remembered as the Father of Australia.

Macquarie receieved strict orders:

Arrest John Macarthur and Major George Johnston for their role in the rebellion against Bligh.

But by the time he arrived in Sydney, both men had already sailed to England to face trial for rebellion against Bligh.

With them gone, Macquarie had one less headache to deal with.

The last three governors had all struggled with the same problem: the New South Wales Corps.

They were unruly, corrupt, and basically running the colony like their personal kingdom.

But Macquarie was different. He came prepared, bringing his own regiment, loyal to him and not corrupted (at least for now).

One of the first actions Macquarie took was to dismantle the NSW Corps and sending them back to England.

Then he replaced them with his troops to maintain social order and enforcement.

Macquarie would go on to govern for 12 years (longer than any of his predecessors), and he left a massive legacy.

In simple terms, he accomplished two big things:

   1. He rebuilt the colony from the ground up.

   2. He gave convicts a genuine second chance in life.

Macquarie began with his expensive infrastructure projects — determined to build a colony that looked more like a civilised city than a prison camp.

One of Macquarie's most ambitious projects was building a grand hospital. The first public hospital in the colony.

The government didn't have the funds for it, so Macquarie got creative.

He made a deal with a few wealthy locals. They'd fund the hospital, and in return, they'd get a special licence to import rum and have monopoly in trading.

The result? A fancy new building and a nickname that stuck: the Rum Hospital.

The hospital consisted of three parts, but the picture below only shows the main central part.

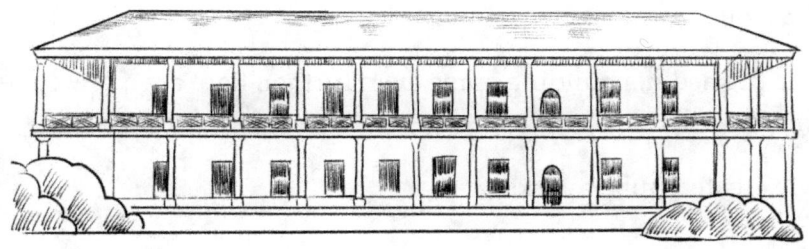

The central part of the Rum Hospital

Fun (and kinda gross) fact: the hospital didn't have toilets (I know, what were they thinking, right?).

So, the staff would just toss the, uh, *contents* of chamber pots right out the window (Yup, literally tossing hygiene out the window).

If you weren't paying attention while walking by, you might end up getting splashed with a *golden* shower.

Today, one of these toilet-less buildings became Parliament House. Another part became Sydney Hospital. Don't worry, it has toilets now.

He pushed his building spree even further, here are a few honourable mentions.

He created public parks.

Hyde Park

He built barracks.

Hyde Barracks

He laid down streets and roads.

He set up a church.

St James' Church

A light house.

Macquarie Lighthouse

To fix the colony's messy economy, he introduced its first official currency, the Holey Dollar and Dump, made by punching a hole in Spanish coins (recycling at its finest!).

The Holey Dollar (left) and Dump (right)

With the new currency came a new bank.

Macquarie established the colony's first bank, the Bank of New South Wales, which over time became today's Westpac.

The Bank of New South Wales

Macquarie founded entire towns and suburbs, like Richmond, Windsor, Bathurst, Wilberforce, Pitt Town, and Castlereagh.

Basically, if you've driven through western Sydney, you've probably been in one of Macquarie's 'startups.'

It's no overstatement to say that without Macquarie, Sydney wouldn't be what it is today.

However, Macquarie's most significant legacy is his Emancipist Policy.

You might be wondering 'What on earth is an emancipist?'

Well, let's break it down.

People who committed crimes and got shipped off to the colony were called convicts (think poor Bob).

But once they served their time, finished their punishment, and legally regained their freedom, they were called emancipists. Essentially, an emancipist = ex-convict. (Convicts who tried to skip their sentence? They were called bushrangers.)

Our stories will be in the next book.

Bushrangers

Even after earning their freedom, emancipists were still treated like second-class citizens.

People looked down on them, judged them by their past, and shut them out of fancy jobs or polite society.

Macquarie strongly believed that every emancipist deserved a fair chance to reintegrate into society. He was ahead of his time in thinking that ex-convicts could be reformed, given the opportunity to rebuild their lives, and be treated with respect.

Macquarie promoted many former convicts to important roles.

People like William Redfern, a convict-turned-respected doctor, and Francis Greenway, the colony's most famous architect, rose to prominence under his leadership.

His wife, Elizabeth Macquarie, shared his views and supported him completely.

Together, they were known for their kindness and fairness, treating everyone with respect, no matter their social class.

Macquarie's attitude made him incredibly popular among the people of Sydney, especially the emancipists who felt valued for the first time. Though his support for ex-convicts earned him many enemies, particularly among the wealthy elite.

These were people who saw themselves as socially superior and wanted nothing to do with ex-convicts. They resented Macquarie for challenging the class system and blurring the line between convict and *gentleman.*

Reverend Samuel Marsden was a prominent political enemy of Macquarie.

In Marsden's eyes, convicts were criminals — full stop. They couldn't be trusted, and they certainly didn't deserve status or respect.

So when Macquarie began offering ex-convicts respect and real opportunities, Marsden was outraged.

He saw Macquarie's policies as a direct attack on the social hierarchy: a system Marsden believed should be led by free settlers and the Church of England, with convicts kept firmly at the bottom.

Marsden had a reputation for harsh punishments. So much so that he earned the nickname 'the Flogging Parson'.

Macquarie wasn't a fan of puishment and tried to curb the brutality, especially in how convicts were treated, but Marsden didn't take kindly to that.

Tensions between them only grew.

Eventually, the British government sent a royal commissioner, John Thomas Bigge (pronounce as *big*, not *beig* or *beeg*) to inspect Macquarie's work in the colony.

The report Bigge produced was far from favourable. He gathered statements from Macquarie's political enemies, many of whom were eager to bring him down, like Samuel Marsden.

Bigge published their accusations back in England, and caused big trouble for Macquarie.

Under mounting pressure from the British government and the weight of Bigge's negative reports, Macquarie was forced to resign as governor in 1821.

He was succeeded by Thomas Brisbane.

Macquarie returned to England, where he spent his final years defending his legacy. Insisting that the criticism against him was unfair and based on misinformation.

He passed away in 1824, but his voice wasn't forgotten. In 1828, his side of the story was finally published, helping to restore his reputation.

Over time, it became clear that — despite the controversies — Macquarie's achievements had shaped the colony in lasting, positive ways. He didn't just govern New South Wales, he re-shaped it for generations to come.

Today, if you're walking through Sydney's CBD, make sure to stop by Hyde Park, where a statue of Lachlan Macquarie stands tall. It was erected in 1908 to honour the man often called the Father of Australia.

Thank you !

www.ingramcontent.com/pod-product-compliance
Lightning Source LLC
LaVergne TN
LVHW051517070426
835507LV00023B/3159